Soulful Nature

A Spiritual Field Guide

Brian Draper and Howard Green

CANTERBURY

PRESS

N o r w i c h

First published in 2020 by the Canterbury Press Norwich
Editorial office
3rd Floor, Invicta House
108–114 Golden Lane
London EC1Y 0TG, UK
www.canterburypress.co.uk

Second impression 2022

Canterbury Press is an imprint of Hymns Ancient & Modern Ltd
(a registered charity)

H
Y Ancient
M & Modern
N
S

Hymns Ancient & Modern® is a registered trademark of
Hymns Ancient & Modern Ltd
13A Hellesdon Park Road, Norwich,
Norfolk NR6 5DR, UK

Acknowledgement is made of poetry under copyright:
'Lent', copyright © 1995 Jean Macdonald Watt, in *A Skirt Without
Pockets*, Geddes & Grosset. Reproduced with permission.
Nadine Swan, 'Pluviophile', www.mirakee.com.
Permission applied for.

Scripture quotations taken from the Holy Bible, New
International Version. Copyright © 1973, 1978, 1984 by
International Bible Society. Used by permission of Hodder &
Stoughton Ltd, a member of Hodder Headline Group.

British Library Cataloguing in Publication data

A catalogue record for this book is available
from the British Library

978 1 78622 147 6

Typeset by Regent Typesetting
Printed and bound in Great Britain by
CPI (Group) UK Ltd

Contents

To our children and grandchildren:
may you savour these places, people and
pathways as much as we have done,
and find yourselves whole, and wholly loved,
here upon God's good Earth.

Foreword

BY ALAN TITCHMARSH MBE

We live in a world where speed is of the essence and where technology occupies the front seat. We have come to rely on technological advances so much that the old adage 'necessity is the mother of invention' has been stood on its head. Nowadays the technocrats invent something and then we have to work out how to use it. The upshot is that we then wonder how on earth we managed without it.

I am not a Luddite, who thinks that every modern invention is a bad one. Far from it: I am writing this on a laptop, my mobile phone is beside me; but alongside it is a fountain pen and through the window is my wildlife pond and wildflower meadow. The natural world is much more important to me and to my physical and spiritual wellbeing than the latest gizmo that enables me to write and broadcast more effectively.

Nature and the great outdoors is my sheet anchor – my deep and true connection with the real world. The worries that are fed to us hourly via news media might take up far more brain space than that view out of the window, but tomorrow they will have evaporated and been replaced with another series of problems and worries which we will feel powerless to influence. The trees and the meadow, the streams and the mountains will remain, provided we have the sense to realize that they need to be cherished and cared for.

I despair at the disconnection that can exist between children and the countryside; that they can name dozens of Pokemon cards (whatever they are) but barely three or four wild flowers or trees – if that. You could dismiss my opinion as the musings of a grumpy old man, but I would argue against that.

Wildlife in all its forms – plants, flowers, trees, animals, birds and insects – have given me more joy since childhood than I can possibly express, and being in their presence in the British countryside affects me deeply. It is something that I cannot adequately put into words, and words are the means by which I earn my living. To cherish the countryside we need to understand it. To understand it is to marvel at it and to love it. To love it and to want to be surrounded by it and to understand the true importance of existence. It really is as simple as that.

As this timely book explains, we need to let nature into our lives and to feel its healing properties. This is not some cranky alternative philosophy; it is the stuff of real life. A day by the sea, the view from the top of a mountain, a walk in the woods or sitting by a river will lift the spirits of even the most dyed-in-the-wool city dweller. We all know that. Each and every one of us needs to make sure that our physical and spiritual connection with nature is nurtured and encouraged. Only then will the planet be in safe hands, and only then will we feel reconciled to the true meaning of life on earth.

Alan Titchmarsh MBE

About the Authors
(in each other's words)

Brian Draper is an experienced retreat leader, author, speaker and creative consultant. He regularly contributes to BBC Radio 4's 'Thought for the Day', and has pioneered the introduction of 'soulful leadership' within organizations. He is an honorary fellow of the University of Winchester.

But for me, Brian has become a spiritual mentor, a walking companion and a close friend. He has helped to open my eyes to a deeper, broader, more contemplative and inclusive form of Christianity. At least I now know the difference between a labyrinth (designed to bring you to its 'centre') and a maze (designed to get you lost)! Brian loves the countryside, and our walks together have enabled me to step back and enjoy the great outdoors in a more holistic way, rather than constantly trying to identify and analyse what I am sensing. However, from time to time I do point out to Brian, who delights in walking through a meadow with bare feet, that ticks may be lurking in the grass! The pleasure of these walks has enabled me to renew an acquaintance with some of the great nature writers and to draw from Brian's rich knowledge of poetry, literature and the best of writing about Christian spirituality. Above all, Brian is a person of integrity who walks the talk, aims to tread lightly on the Earth and is full to overflowing with love and compassion for others. I have learned so much.

Howard Green was trained as a botanist, becoming a teacher and then a secondary head teacher. Later he moved into leadership development and educational research. He now volunteers as an outdoor guide with the National Trust at Mottisfont in Hampshire and enjoys the benefits of retirement, including his grandchildren and, as a complete novice, exploring local history.

But beyond that, Howard is one of those rare souls that you count yourself truly blessed to have encountered; a fount not just of knowledge, but of wisdom. A kind and caring fellow traveller, who will usually have an answer to your question about when the migrating birds arrive, or what kind of leaf this is ... but will always go away and find the answer if he doesn't. That spirit of enquiry has poured through his own spiritual search, too. He has faced tragedy in his own life, which has served to deepen his compassion for, and connection with, the world around him, yielding a strongly gentle, wise and deepening form of Christian spirituality that is able to hold the paradoxes of life with loving care within his heart. To top it all off, he usually comes armed with a flask of coffee and a Tupperware of flapjacks, which makes him just about the perfect travelling companion!

The 'South Country'

A word about the area in which we walked

Our selection of twelve places to walk has been inspired by some of the great nature writers, from the late eighteenth century through to the present day. Among them is Edward Thomas, who found particular solace in walking what he called the 'South Country'. This is also the title of one of Thomas's books, in which he acknowledges that the phrase came from a poem by Hilaire Belloc, who would dream of 'The great hills of the South Country' when living in the Midlands.

Thomas explains that for him the South Country 'includes the counties of Kent, Sussex, Surrey, Hampshire, Berkshire, Wiltshire, Dorset and part of Somerset. East and west across (the South Country) go ranges of chalk hills, their sides smoothly hollowed by Nature, or sharply scored by old roads. On their lower slopes they carry the chief woods of the south country.' Although we have not walked in all these counties, we have at least seen them from various vantage points on the chalk hills along the way.

We also decided to walk in three urban areas: Romsey and Winchester in Hampshire and Salisbury in Wiltshire; all with great churches or cathedrals. Most of us now live in towns or cities and we'd love our readers to explore green spaces on their doorsteps without necessarily having to drive anywhere. And we had a strong urge to see the sea, so we included a visit to the Jurassic Coast in Dorset.

The directions at the back of the book will hopefully get

you to the twelve places and provide an outline of where we walked. However, we would be delighted if you made each walk your own by getting a paper map (we used the Ordnance Survey Explorer series), creating some diversions and researching places of interest along the way. Or, perhaps like Edward Thomas, you would prefer just to follow your nose, sniffing out interesting new places that might appear unexpectedly on the journey. Our routes were not long, typically two or three miles, and those who prefer to stride out for longer distances can plan their own extensions, maybe integrating one of these walks into a few days away. But some words of warning: if you walk too fast you will miss much, and we urge you to pause regularly to enjoy the view! Finally, why not turn your phone off, or set it to silent, while you walk, and take your headphones out of your ears? In that way, you'll be much better placed to give Nature your undivided and loving attention.

Introduction

What's not to love? Twelve inspiring walks, one a month, through delightful countryside, in soulful company. Walking, talking, and deepening the relationship, not just with each other, but with nature, and God.

In fact, we've loved it so much that we'd like to share this journey with you!

We have been guiding outdoor retreats together for several years. We began with the idea that Howard – outdoor guide at the National Trust's Mottisfont Abbey, with expert knowledge of flora and fauna – would help others to learn more about the natural world, while Brian would provide the 'spiritual' interludes: times to pause, to breathe, to reconnect more deeply with a place, and God, and our true self.

What emerged between us was a conversation, and an exploration, about how to engage meaningfully within nature, which we've shared with so many people of all sorts of different backgrounds (and perspectives) along the way: seeking wisdom *together* about what it means to be truly part of the 'whole':

Part of creation.
Part of the beauty.
Part of the tangle.
Part of the rhythms and seasons.
Part of a higher, wider, deeper Presence.
Part of a spiritual flow through our Christian faith.
Part of the problem, as humans, at this time of climate crisis
and mass extinction.
And, please God, part of the solution.

We planned twelve walks, to get outside into different contexts (some urban), to notice what happens outside through the months, the seasons, the year, and to take our place within it. To walk without agenda, but instead to be *present*, and to use all our senses. To smell the bluebells, to feel the smooth bark of a thousand-year yew, to taste the blackberry from the hedge, to listen for the song of the skylark, to watch for the dazzle of a kingfisher. For this is no senseless journey; in fact, it's truly sensuous.

This book records those walks, the conversations that flowed, the silences that spoke louder, the trees we've rested against, the pathways (often truly ancient) that we've followed, and the people who have gone before us – nature writers, scientists and naturalists who have pioneered ways of cultivating friendship with the natural world, with compassion, observation, poetry and love.

We wanted to maintain the distinction of our own two voices within the text, as this book is an expression of our ongoing conversation on our walks. So for clarity, Howard's sections are in italics, and Brian's are in the regular roman text.

We don't expect you to come and repeat our walks (although we've given directions, if you would like to!), but instead we hope you'll be inspired to discover the places and the people in your own area of the country that can nurture a richer sense of being.

* * *

We agree with Gerald May, the much-loved American psychiatrist and theologian, who once wrote, 'We have been fractured … broken off from the nature of our world, broken away from the nature of one another, broken apart from our own nature …'

When we go in search of the soul of nature, we discover more of our own soulful nature in the process. Beyond the driven, short-termist, consumerist and toxic patterns of contemporary life – which are intensified by the constant chattering and frequently anxious inner monologue of the ego – there are different, unforced rhythms to discover. A flow. A way of being that embraces the decay and darkening of the autumn and winter months, as much as the warmth and wonder of our spring and summer days.

When you step into nature, and if you give it a little time, you can feel different. Reset. Restored. Healed, oftentimes. But we find it hard to say why. Something profound is happening to us, when we walk on a beach, or climb a hill, or watch a river flow – but it's so hard to put into words that it often goes unsaid, and thus neglected.

The brilliant nature writer Robert Macfarlane has lamented powerfully the loss, among children, of a basic vocabulary for nature. Words such as blackberry, acorn and kingfisher have been dropped from the *Oxford Junior Dictionary* in favour of terms about social media and IT, which are in more common parlance. And without those words, we lose our connection with a world that will disappear faster *because* of that lack of connection.

We've noticed that our culture struggles, too, to find words for the relationship we can – and must – nurture with creation, if we are truly to become part of the solution at this fragile and perilous time for habitats, species and climate. Wisdom words such as awakening, presence, rootedness, growth, fruitfulness, wholeness, Spirit, soulfulness ...

This book explores, and hopefully expresses, something more of that relationship – the soul friendship – we may culti-vate, between humanity, the Earth and its Creator. If we inspire you simply to step outside, to breathe the air, and to establish that friendship for yourself, we will not have walked in vain.

Make yourself a flask, and please feel most welcome to join us.

Go well.

Brian Draper
Howard Green

January
Stories from Deep Time

A trip to the Dorset seaside and the Jurassic Coast

A lorry has overturned on the nearby M3 in the morning rush hour, and diverted traffic is disgorging through Winchester's back streets. It's gridlock, and as my daughter and I cycle our way through the fumes on the school run, it's as if everyone's trying desperately to get somewhere, but getting nowhere, fast ...

Happy New Year.

It also means I'm running late to collect Howard for our first outing. The adrenaline's pumping, as it does when you're against the clock and there's nothing you can do about it. 'Just breathe deep, and stay calm,' Howard says with a broad telephone smile, when I call him. It works. In fact, it works every time:

Breathe deep.

* * *

In the fullness of time, I'm picking him up, late but now un-rushed, and we're off to the Dorset seaside. What better way to cleanse the palette at the start of the year than to visit the sea? The salty breeze, the churn of water, that uplifting quality of light that seems to bounce off the waves when the sun comes out, flooding the sky with brilliance ... It helps you to believe that a fresh start is possible.

We're heading for Kimmeridge Bay, via the scenic route, to enjoy a ride on the Sandbanks chain ferry which crosses the short but treacherous stretch of water at the mouth of Poole Harbour. For a few brief minutes you're on deck drinking in the deep blue-greens and foaming whites of sea and sky, and it's as if you are heading through a gateway into another world: the tree-lined Dorset-shire land of Enid Blyton, who lived just along the way in the village of Studland.

Brownsea Island (or 'Whispering Island', as she called it) is on our right, where the Scouting movement began and where red squirrels cling tenaciously to life as they would a pine tree, protected by the waters of Poole Harbour from their scurrilous grey cousins.

It's as if much of Dorset has been protected by these waters, and by its relative remoteness, and by the army ranges which have effectively frozen large tracts of land in time since they were requisitioned during World War Two. Old paint-peeled phone boxes still way-mark the narrow lanes, as gentle reminders of other times, other ways.

The road picks up after the ferry spews you off, Jonah-like, on to the Studland side of the harbour, and from here it's a snaking drive to Corfe, where the gaunt ruins of its famous castle stand as proudly as they can at a gap in the Purbeck Hills; and which my son, as a two-year-old, christened 'Oh Dear Castle', which always sounds better to me.

Then, on towards Kimmeridge, the January sun belying the storm that pounded the South Country yesterday. A welcome relief, after seemingly endless days of bruising grey. It's not always an easy time of the year.

* * *

The hundred miles from Studland Bay and Swanage to Exmouth in east Devon are now recognized as a World Heritage Site, called the Jurassic Coast. Erosion by wave action and the weather has exposed an almost continuous sequence of rock formations that span 185 million years of geological history. At different times in the past, this area has been desert, shallow tropical sea and marsh; and the fossilized remains of the various creatures that lived in these diverse habitats have been preserved in the rocks.

Kimmeridge is a small village nestled in a valley that descends gently to the sea at Kimmeridge Bay. Today, the welcome sunlight seems to intensify the mellow ochre tones of its picture-postcard cottages. A few plants in well-tended gardens and on dry-stone walls are showing the first colours of the year: crocuses, daffodils and early primroses in sheltered places.

At the centre of the village is a new building, built with local Purbeck limestone and housing the Museum of Jurassic Marine Life, otherwise known as 'The Etches Collection'. Steve Etches is a former plumber who has spent the last 35 years scouring the rocks of this one bay. During his epic and single-minded pursuit, he has discovered over 2,500 fossils, many of them species new to science. As a fitting reward for his achievements, geologists around the world have coined the term 'Kimmeridgian' for rocks of this age (150 million years). It's an extraordinary story of what one person can achieve – all without the advantage of a formal academic education.

The museum itself is a single large space with displays along both its sides. At one end, through a glass divide, the man himself can often be seen intently leaning over a bench in his workshop. He uses tools that are more familiar in a dentist's surgery to slowly and carefully excavate the form of an ancient creature from its encasing rock.

Overhead, a massive screen has various fish and reptiles swimming to and fro. You can imagine sitting on the sea-bed of that warm Jurassic ocean, but a warning: you'd do this at considerable risk of being eaten alive by a hungry pliosaur, up to 15 metres long and with lots of sharp teeth! Fortunately there was an abundance of marine life available as alternative food and several of the fossil fish on display are exquisite examples of Steve's meticulous art of restoration. Each one has hundreds of small bones and teeth, eyes and fins, all exposed in amazing detail.

It's also clear that the scientists who named these fossils had great fun and created some real tongue-twisters. There are fish called Leptolepis and Thrissops; a squid named Trachyteuthis; a local reptile called Kimmerosaurus and – try this one! – the memorable Torvoneustes coryphaeus, which looks like a cross between a crocodile and a dolphin. For those in the know, these names all have descriptive meanings, usually derived from Greek or Latin.

Living for the longer term

There's a quote from Etches on the wall, which immediately grabs my attention:

> 'As fossil collectors ... if we are to build on our past discoveries, we must collaborate with our contemporaries to unlock the "stories from deep time".'

Deep time! What a thought. It's a concept introduced by the eighteenth-century Scottish geologist James Hutton to help us begin to wrap our minds around the great age of the Earth, now reckoned to be around 4.5 billion years (and beyond that, the age of the universe, another 10 billion years older still).

The author John McPhee (in *Basin and Range*) paints a lovely picture to explain how deep time relates to us, to humanity: if you consider Earth's history as the old measure of the English yard, he says – the distance from the king's nose to the tip of his outstretched hand – then 'one stroke of a nail file on his middle finger erases human history'.

I recall my anxiety at being late this morning. We keep accelerating 'time' – life has become one long rush – to the detriment of our health, our wellbeing and our relationships. Deep time whispers through its deafening silence of a different pace and rhythm at work within the natural progression of life.

I think of Steve Etches, slowly, lovingly excavating fossils, welcoming them back meticulously into the light, bone by bone; a little like a contemporary Michelangelo, calling forth with a chisel the shape of life from a block of stone; bringing forgotten stories back from the depths.

* * *

When we live just for the short-term – at perpetually high speed – we're heading for a crash, personally and collectively. Humans may have shown up late to the party, yet already we have, in a geological instant, set in motion the sixth great extinction of species (the fifth was around 65 million years ago, when the dinosaurs disappeared).

The key to a change, to 'recovery', as the environmental activist and 'deep ecology' writer Joanna Macy puts it in *Active Hope*, is to have 'a larger view of time'; to see that our daily actions have consequences that will outlast us, for ill, or for good, as Macy explains:

> We can bring deep time to mind as we go about our daily lives. Even as we wash the dishes, pay the bills, go to meetings, and so on, we can school ourselves to be aware, now and then, of the hosts of ancestral and future beings surrounding us like a cloud of witnesses.

Macy encourages us, as an exercise, to think of someone seven generations forward, 200 years or so in the future. 'Imagine what they'd say to you. Open your mind, and listen,' she says. 'The vast story of our planet [can] imbue the most ordinary acts with meaning and purpose. Each of us is an intrinsic part of that story, like a cell in a larger organism. And in this story, each of us has a role to play.'

An inspiring woman

Speaking of which, the story of Steve Etches reminds us of the most famous fossil hunter of the Jurassic Coast, Mary Anning. She provides an inspirational example of a woman whose work – within what was so restrictively a 'man's world' – was ground-breaking. It laid the foundations early in the nineteenth century for the new sciences of geology and palaeontology, and Anning is today celebrated as one of the most influential women in the history of science.

She was born just along the coast at Lyme Regis in Dorset in 1799. Mary was one of ten children, yet only she and her brother Joseph survived into adulthood. In fact, her survival has been described as a miracle. She was a sickly baby and, while she was being looked after by friends one summer, the party was sheltering under a tree during a violent thunderstorm. Tragically, they were struck by lightning and only Mary survived.

As a hobby, Mary's father Richard collected fossils along the Lyme Regis shoreline, cleaning them in his workshop and offering them for sale to tourists from a table outside the family's cottage. Mary was a constant companion for Richard on his often dangerous escapades. The cliffs along this section of coast are notoriously unstable, and Richard suffered a fall himself. He died prematurely (in part from his injuries) in 1810, leaving the family in debt and without a provider. The mantle of fossil collector passed to Mary and by the 1820s she had turned a hobby into a family business and opened a shop.

She discovered many remarkable fossils, including several complete ichthyosaur skeletons and one of the first plesiosaurs – fearsome hunters of the Jurassic seas. These specimens were embedded in large slabs of rock and Mary had to organize extra help to drag them back to her workshop. She then spent many hours extracting the fossilized remains, without the use of modern power tools, and sold the best examples to wealthy collectors from across Europe (who often took the credit for the discoveries).

She eventually died of cancer in 1847 at the relatively young age of 48. It's ironic that she did not live long enough to hear about the publication in 1859 of Charles Darwin's book On the Origin of Species. *His theory of evolution challenged the traditional Christian teaching that the Earth was created in six days. Darwin drew on evidence from geology and palaeontology, concluding that the Earth's history went back millions of years and that fossils are the remains of extinct plants and animals from much earlier times.*

Despite discovering many of these fossils herself, Mary remained a firm Christian believer throughout her life and was a regular member of the congregation at her local church. Perhaps her inquisitive nature enabled her to be more open-minded about the implications of her discoveries, and would have prepared her for the much longer time scales of life on Earth that would be described in the palaeontological evidence for Darwin's theory.

Where spirituality and science meet and embrace

I wonder what we might learn from the idea that God didn't necessarily create the world in six days flat with a click of the fingers? For some, the discovery of deep time implies that science and religion should never mix. Yet it doesn't have to be this way, especially if you see the first passages of the Bible as they were intended, as the most profound *poetic* reflection on the relationship between God and creation.

This was something appreciated by the Jesuit priest, geologist and paleontologist Pierre Teilhard de Chardin, who didn't see incompatibility but the potential for yet deeper *communion* – a relationship of mutual flourishing – between the spiritual and scientific worlds; and between (at the most profound level) 'Spirit' and 'matter'.

He was the rarest of breeds, a scientist and a mystic, who felt most fully alive in the material world – within the world of nature, as so many of us do. So he was convinced that the spiritual life was not about escaping the material (as is so often taught in religions), but in finding God right there, at the heart of it all: 'the divine radiating from the depths of blazing matter'.

* * *

I love the implications – that if this beautiful world, within this incredible universe, has a Creator, then this Creator takes their time – their deepest time – within it all. They don't sit aloof upon on a throne above in judgement; neither do they live exclusively 'in our heart', squeezed from every other public space by rational knowledge. Instead, God is the One in whom we live and move and have our being. Creation is happening, still, because God is happening.

And while a tree is not God, God's DNA is in the tree, and in the birds that rest within it, and in the clouds above it, and in the earth below it, and in the person resting against its trunk, savouring some moments of divine reconnection ...

What privilege! Our human ability to reflect consciously and connect spiritually, soulfully, while resting against a tree, for example, or swimming in the sea, or skiing down a mountainside, is unique in the (known) universe, and an incredibly recent plot development within the story of deep time, too. Yet it's surely a crucial part *of* that story. We're invited to awaken, to open our blinking eyes to the dawning light, to breathe the air and stand up straight and bear witness to this miraculous context in which we find ourselves. To smell, taste, see, hear, *feel* our way deeper into the mysteries and wonders of life itself.

As the eco-theologian Thomas Berry (who loved the work of Teilhard) puts it in *Evening Thoughts*, 'Within the universe, the planet Earth, with all its wonder, is the place for the meeting of the divine and the human.'

The Bible evokes a beautiful image, of the Spirit of God 'hovering over the waters', way back in the beginning, before creation was set in motion. It has taken a long, long time for us to get here, but we are part of the gentle unfolding of a masterpiece.

'Above all, trust in the slow work of God,' writes Teilhard.

'Only God could say what this new Spirit gradually forming in you will be.'

We are a work in progress. That same Spirit hovers over the waters of our own, personal beginning, I believe. Perhaps that's why our soul stirs when we stand beside the sea, and watch.

This is the sea

It is less than a mile down the valley from the village to Kimmeridge Bay, following a footpath known as the Hardy Way (Thomas Hardy courted his first love, Eliza Nicholl, down here). We descend the steep steps on to the beach and celebrate reaching the sea, captivated by the swooshing sound of the waves on the pebbles in a stiff westerly breeze and inhaling that invigorating smell, now known to be caused by tiny molecules of gas released by bacteria and called dimethyl sulphide (not ozone, despite what your mother might have told you).

On the cliff top to the east sits the squat Clavell Tower, an observatory and folly built in 1830. It has literary associations both with Hardy and as the setting for the crime writer P. D. James' novel, The Black Tower. *To the west a red flag flutters in the wind, signifying that the Lulworth Firing Ranges are being used by the army today, though we can't hear any gunshots or exploding munitions. Beyond the flag, the cliffs rise majestically towards Lulworth and on to the misty horizon where we can just make out the promontory of Portland Bill, jutting into the sea. This feels like a special place. Perhaps 'Kimmeridgian' is a word that should be used to describe more than just the rocks and fossils. How about broadening its meaning to 'stories from deep time'?*

The low cliffs behind the beach are composed of relatively soft Kimmeridge Clay interleaved with harder bands of limestone. The harder layers are like the pages of a book about Jurassic marine life. As one works down the cliff face, each layer contains successively older fossils. The lowest visible bands of limestone run out into the sea forming what are known as the

'Kimmeridge Ledges'. They are clearly visible at low tide and walking across the ledges prompts regular 'wow' moments, as the contours of large ammonites and other creatures appear beneath your feet.

Slow but continuous erosion by constant wave action helps to create a fossil hunter's paradise, which is why Steve Etches has never needed to travel further than this particular bay. Evidence for the fragility of the cliffs and the power of erosion is clearly apparent: a pill-box, once on the cliff top and in use as a wartime guard-house, has been unceremoniously dumped on the beach as the cliff has collapsed. In the 2000s and at a cost of almost £900,000, Clavell Tower was moved just 25 metres inland to prevent it from falling into the sea. It was a mammoth project that involved taking apart and then reconstructing over 16,000 stones.

The stillness between two waves of the sea

'What are your thoughts, as you look out onto the ocean? What do you see?' asks Thomas Berry.

Howard and I choose to spend an extended time of stillness by the water, watching. He wanders along the shoreline. I stay here at the base of this short cliff. The sun is out, and it brightens my face, and warms my back through the rocks upon which I lean. This is a blessing, and here there is no rush.

Here is stillness.

* * *

T. S. Eliot writes, in his poem 'Little Gidding', of 'the stillness between two waves of the sea'.

There is a stillness that lies behind all things, that sits within these timelessly breaking waves before us. A stillness nevertheless in harmony with the motion of the waves, which together create a rhythm that has pulsed since the first burst of divine energy, way back in the beginning; a rhythm that is marking deep time for us, still.

As you breathe, and relax, and watch, and listen, perhaps you notice something of that rhythm pulsing through you, like a heartbeat.

* * *

And here I am, leaning on the clay between two distinct layers of limestone, layers that seem to ripple up the cliff like waves. I'm no geologist; I need a Steve Etches or a Howard Green to tell me whether I'm in the Jurassic or Triassic here, and how many millions of years separate the six feet (2 m) or so between one layer and the next ... but this is deep time in cross-section, and time seems to deepen in this moment for me, as I wait. It is compressed by its own sheer weight, yet speaks of abundance, expansion, volume.

* * *

An elderly couple wander by, his hair as bright as white horses; dignified, hands in the pockets of a great coat, trimmed beard, bending to reach for a fossil, scouring, searching.

He skims a stone. Perhaps this is where he came as a child; I have played skimmers with my own children here. I can remember my dad teaching me how to skim stones too, and for a moment I can imagine Dad's dad teaching him, and the generations seem to back up with each flat bounce of the old man's throw.

We reach a long way back. We reach a long way forward. The cloud of witnesses seems close. Stories weave between us, within us.

* * *

Howard approaches, carrying his camping chair (which for today's purpose is a 'meditation stool'). He stops, stares out to sea. I can't see what he sees; but his wife Jan, he tells me, loves the waves, and she uses them as her 'centring image'; so perhaps he's centring himself now, with her and his family, and God, within this pulsing stillness.

This seems like a healing place. When we find healing, we also become a healing for the world around us.

And then, as if to break the stillness, Howard smashes a rock as a Greek might smash crockery after a meal, searching for ammonites to take home to Jan, a keepsake to show that we kept this day well.

Flotsam and jetsam

Since the broadcast of Sir David Attenborough's iconic Blue Planet 2 *TV series, the oceans seem to have flooded the public consciousness, especially with such powerful footage of plastic pollution, in its many sickening forms, threatening so much marine wildlife. It is very good news that, in recent days, 41 marine conservation zones have been designated in England alone, to add to 50 existing sites. This will ensure a network of protected areas in our seas, which include cold water corals, forests of sea fans, rocky canyons and sandbanks – 'an astonishingly varied range of submerged landscapes and habitats which support the stunning diversity of marine life found in the UK', according to the Wildlife Trusts. The conservation zone along this Purbeck coast includes a critical black sea bream nesting ground, rare beds of maerl (a hardened seaweed), and vital habitat for threatened species such as stalked jellyfish and peacock's tail seaweed.*

The beach at Kimmeridge is pleasingly clean, but four small objects become the focus of my attention. The first two are a short piece of plastic rope about four inches (10 cm) long, probably trimmed and thrown overboard by a local crab fisherman; and, of similar length, the root of a giant kelp, a brown seaweed that grows in deep water. Both are symbols of strength. The rope is made from three strands woven together and resonates with words of wisdom in the Bible, that 'a cord of three strands is not quickly broken'. Much can be overcome in life with a soul-friend and with God.

The main root of the kelp has a cluster of shorter rootlets at the bottom, each terminating in a flattened knob which glues the seaweed to a rock. This natural method of securing a kelp to the ocean floor is surprisingly resilient, able to withstand the forces of the most powerful storms.

But storms will have their victims, and the other two objects speak of fragility: the skeleton and feathers of a young seagull washed up on the pebbles; and an exquisite, delicately divided frond of red seaweed that has been torn from a rock pool by the surging waves of a high tide.

As we leave the beach, we split open another slab of rock to reveal a host of tiny fossils, including several small ammonites, and hope that there will still be (perhaps different) wildlife here in another 150 million years.

* * *

We're thrilled when we find a few ammonites in the rocks that Howard breaks open. I want to pass them on. My daughter loves rocks, and hoped I would bring her home a fossil.

I want to pass *this* on.

We might call deep time 'the eternal'. It's all picture language, really (as I often tell my kids). And it strikes me that we don't have to wait for eternity to begin. Instead, eternity waits for us, waits for us to show up here, and to stand upon the shore of our life, and to remember the story of which we are part.

The temperature drops, and the light is trying to fade, just as it faded on the day this ammonite in my hand fell to the sea floor and began its rest. This ammonite, which last felt the sun's rays 150 million years ago, until today.

A cormorant dives into the spume.

Above, slender layers of stratified cloud mirror the waves lining up in the bay, which in turn mirror the layers of limestone in the cliffs. Lines flow and blur between sea and sky and land, in communion.

Billiard-green hills and fields, a row of fishermen's cottages, and pied wagtails bobbing on the cliff top above.

Your favourite place on Earth

Leaving Kimmeridge, we are delighted to see the first lambs of the year skipping and frolicking in the sunlit fields along-side the road; and we then drive north past the tiny hamlet of Steeple, up on to the ridge of the Purbeck Hills.

It is a glorious late January evening and, with the slightly longer hours of daylight, we decide to walk the short distance along a green road to the summit of the Stonehill Down Nature Reserve.

An old stone signpost, partly hidden in the undergrowth, informs us that Tyneham village is three and a half miles to the west. No doubt many villagers from Tyneham walked this way in the centuries before their homes were requisitioned by the War Office in 1943, so that the surrounding land could be used for D-Day preparations.

The last person to leave Tyneham stuck a notice to the church door: 'Please treat the church and houses with care; we have given up our homes where many of us lived for generations to help win the war to keep men free. We shall return one day and thank you for treating the village kindly.' These displaced people, their children and grandchildren are still waiting to return to Tyneham.

But our thoughts are not melancholic; this is a time and a place to reflect on the day and to lift our spirits. We stand at the top with the wind in our hair and the chill sunlight on our faces drinking in the panoramic views. The light and the shadows seem to create a moving landscape of soft green valleys and hills set against a backdrop of the surging waters of Kimmeridge Bay in the distance.

Up here you feel strangely part of the surrounding earth, sea and sky. We become more aware of the scene before us as a temporary pause in the processes of deep time that have changed and sculpted the Earth's surface: the slow churning motion of tectonic plates, the sudden eruption of volcanoes, seismic shifts in the underlying rocks, profound changes to the climate and to the plants and animals living here. We have been blessed to live in a period of extended settlement for these

*natural processes, and, at this precise moment in time, an expe-
rience of deep peace.*

*The words of the psalmist seem like a perfect benediction,
at the start of another new year which can quickly fill with so
many short-term anxieties:*

> *Lord, you have been our dwelling-place throughout all gener-
> ations. Before the mountains were born or you brought forth
> the earth and the world, from everlasting to everlasting you
> are God ... For a thousand years in your sight are like a day
> that has just gone by.*
> *(Psalm 90.1–4)*

* * *

This, I declare to Howard, is my favourite view on Earth. (I
wonder, which is yours?) A song-thrush serenades my decision,
an early sign of nature's reawakening from its winter dormancy.

If we stayed here long enough, we would start to see the
stars. The farthest object you can see with the unaided eye is a
galaxy far, far away – Andromeda, to be precise, 2.5 million
light years off, its faint beams as ancient as the days when
hominids began walking this earth. Waves still pulsing with
the light of life.

It's all too much to take in, really – whether that's the mag-
nitude of deep time, or the magnificence of space, or indeed
simply the sheer wonder of this view, which is impossible to
distill or 'capture'. It's a mystery, and that's part of the beauty:
to be part of this mystery, too. As Thomas Berry (in *Selected
Writings*) puts it, 'We bear the universe in our beings as the
universe bears us in its being. The two have a total presence to
each other and to that deeper mystery out of which both the
universe and ourselves have emerged.'

We can't stay here all night, however. Not because we don't
have time; there seems to be more of it than ever, somehow. But
my in-laws live close by, and they've promised us a cup of tea
and a slice of apple cake. Food for the body, food for the soul.

The stars, like time itself, will wait.

Activities

- Notice the way you drive. Try to slow yourself down a little. Be mindful: notice your hands on the steering wheel, be aware of what you can see and hear around you, and try to take a journey where you do not get lost in thought or caught up in the rush. Use Howard's words, 'Just breathe deep and stay calm', to help you arrive at your destination unrushed.

- In the light of deep time, see if you can find fresh perspectives on your own life and priorities, perhaps identifying areas of life where you could behave differently and find a new balance. One simple way to gain a little perspective is to ask, 'Will this matter in five years' time?' And if it won't, try to stop worrying about it now.

- Visit a favourite place by the sea and spend time meditating on the line from T. S. Eliot's poem 'Little Gidding', 'the stillness between two waves of the sea', considering ways to find moments of stillness in the rush of normal life. You might also like to do some beachcombing (perhaps filling a bag with plastic rubbish as you go) – and let a few of the most interesting objects that you find tell their stories and speak into your life.

- Reflect on the biblical Creation account in Genesis 1 and Genesis 2.1–3 in particular. What can you learn from the poetry of the writing, about the communion between God and creation, Spirit and matter, people and the Earth? What phrases or words do you notice afresh? Try to rest in the 'goodness' that God saw in his creation, including human beings, and be reassured of that goodness within you.

- Use Pierre Teilhard de Chardin's words as a meditation upon the pace of your own life: 'Above all, trust in the slow work of God ... and *accept the anxiety of feeling yourself in suspense and incomplete.*'

- Think about a descendant, seven generations on, who will be here in 200 years' time. 'Imagine what they'd say to you. Open your mind, and listen,' as Joanna Macy advises.
- What would you say to *them*? You might also like to try writing a letter about the story we find ourselves in, here in the twenty-first century, and how you are playing your part within it.
- Visit your favourite view whenever you have the opportunity, reflect on why it is so special to you and give thanks for the whole of God's creation, perhaps by reading your favourite psalm of praise.

2

February
Finding Rhythm

*A visit to the parish of Selborne, home to
the great naturalist Gilbert White*

THE parish of SELBORNE lies in the extreme eastern corner
of the county of Hampshire, bordering on the county of
Sussex, and not far from the county of Surrey ... The high
part to the south-west consists of a vast hill of chalk, rising
three hundred feet (91.4 m) above the village; and is divided
into a sheep down, the high wood, and a long hanging wood
called The Hanger. The covert of this eminence is altogether
beech, the most lovely of all forest trees, whether we consider
its smooth rind or bark, its glossy foliage, or graceful pendulous boughs. The down, or sheep-walk, is a pleasing park-
like spot, of about one mile by half that space, jutting out on
the verge of the hill-country, where it begins to break down
into the plains, and commanding a very engaging view ...

* * *

So begins *The Natural History and Antiquities of Selborne*, by Gilbert White – one of the most influential natural history books ever to be written, and all set within one single, charming parish in southern England.

White's book has been in print ever since it was published in 1789, and along the way has profoundly influenced figures as diverse as the scientist Charles Darwin, the philosopher Henry David Thoreau and the poet John Clare. It is also one of the principal sources of inspiration for our present-day flood of nature writers.

Given that Selborne lies in our patch of the South Country, it's hard for us to resist a visit. White's biographer, the ecologist Richard Mabey, assures his readers that 'there is no need to view [Selborne] through the glass of nostalgia or pastoral whimsy, because you can touch the actual stuff of Gilbert White's writings'. Delightfully, the area remains largely unchanged, aside from the inevitable increase in through-traffic, and we sense this trip will speak not just of deeper time, but of place.

In the short ride from Winchester to Selborne, along the shamefully litter-strewn A31 – plastic is entangled in seemingly every bare hedge along the main road, and flaps in the breeze like a ghostly lament – Howard explains more about the man who learned to watch nature like a hawk; who recorded the details of what he saw, every day, for decades; and who, by staying rooted principally in one locality, discerned with patient reverence the recurring seasonal patterns of the natural world around him.

The sacramental rhythms of time and place

Gilbert White was born in Selborne in 1720, died there in 1793, and spent most of his life there in between. He was a curate (never a vicar) in the parish church, did not marry and has no known portrait, so we don't know what he looked like. His fame is based instead on a remarkable correspondence with friends which continued over several decades, and which became his book.

The book itself includes what might first appear to be rather tedious lists of the seasonal events affecting more than 400 species of plants and animals. White gathered his information in Selborne, in partnership with another naturalist, William Markwick, who did the same at Battle, Sussex, between 1768 and 1793.

For 25 years, day after day, they painstakingly recorded when, for example, the first flowers bloomed, and field mushrooms appeared, and lambs were born; even when moles were 'throwing up little hillocks' (or starting their spring-cleaning, as Beatrix Potter was later to imagine!). White also kept meticulous weather records.

Through their acute observation of the seasons, White and Markwick became the founding fathers of phenology – the science of natural cycles and seasonal changes, particularly in relation to climate and its impact on plant and animal life. Their apparently dry lists of data provided a ground-breaking source of scientific information, and subsequently a major source of evidence for the influence of human activity on climate change.

* * *

My in-laws have kept a 'nature diary' for many years in Dorset, tracking dates for the return of migrating birds to their garden, and the peeping up of the first spring flowers, and the sighting of butterflies – and it's plain to see how attuned they are to the ebb and flow of creation. It deepens them, as they go deeper into the place where they live. And it's fascinating to note how, so often, it's to the *day* that a particular type of bird, for example, makes its reappearance.

Interestingly, with the climate emergency now upon us, and 'nature's calendar' subtly but significantly starting to shift, the Woodland Trust is seeking help from the public for its long-established phenology research project, asking us to watch for particular signs throughout the year: for example, with trees, the first budburst, the first leaf, the first fruits, and so on – all on the same tree. You can watch for amphibians in the pond in your park, the ash tree you walk past on the way to work, grasses in the field where you walk your dog, birds and insects in your garden ... The idea is to continue to build evidence for how recent weather affects wildlife, and how climate change affects timings in nature (for more details, see the activities on page 36).

Here, on a shivery morning in Selborne, we're mindful, too, as we near the village, of the *spiritual* cycles embedded within our changing seasons – which, at their richest, are a soulful human response to where we find ourselves within the natural rhythms of creation. We're not long past Candlemas, which falls on 2 February and overlays a pre-Christian festival called Imbolc. Imbolc marked the Celtic beginning of spring, and fires were lit to celebrate the strengthening of the light at this equidistant point between the winter solstice and the spring equinox.

Candlemas, or 'the Feast of the Presentation' as it's also known, is one of the oldest Christian feast days, dating back to the fourth century. It marks the time when the baby Jesus was 'presented' at the temple (according to Jewish custom), 40 days after Christmas. Candles were (and often still are) blessed in churches, and then lit at home, to welcome the coming of 'the light of the world'. It's a reminder to me, at the fag end of winter, that the wonder of Christmas doesn't have to end when we take down the decorations; the humble lighting of a candle at any time can reconnect us with the sense of light, hope and promise that begins at Advent with the revolutionary idea that the Creator 'became flesh and dwelled among us' (John 1).

Richard Mabey suggests, returning to Gilbert White, that phenology describes not just a set of factual observations about nature, but a sacred sense of the 'kindredness of living things' within a whole community. There's something sacramental, he says, about the ordinary dramas of courtship, birth, survival and migration 'that are played out in its woods and fields'. It also positively diminishes our human egocentricity, for human wholeness is surely only achieved in relation to the whole of creation, our kin.

White's book wasn't an immediate 'hit' when it was published, but it began to strike a popular chord in the first half of the nineteenth century, thanks especially to the sense of place it evoked, at a time when the Industrial Revolution was uprooting so many ordinary people from rural life and their proximity to the land.

Rural life was incredibly hard, of course, and there's no need to cultivate a false nostalgia; yet its ever-turning seasons at least earthed us, as people; and surely those rhythms call to us, still, from deep within our place of exile; from that place of dislocation where we can buy un-fragrant strawberries any time of day or night from the supermarket, even in February.

Grooves of ancient presence

The final steep descent in the car from the chalk uplands into Selborne and the surrounding wooded valleys reveals a partially hidden landscape of fast-flowing streams, small fields and sunken tracks.

White describes the 'hollow lanes' of Selborne as one of the 'singularities of this place':

> *These roads are, by the traffic of ages and the fretting of water, worn down so that they look more like water-courses than roads. In many places they are reduced sixteen or eighteen feet (5.4 m) beneath the level of the fields; and after floods and in frosts, exhibit very grotesque and wild appearances, from the tangled roots that are twisted among the strata, and from the torrents rushing down their broken sides; and especially when these cascades are frozen into icicles, hanging in all the fanciful shapes of frost-work.*

The hollow lanes were also the main routes out to the surrounding towns and villages, and until roads were metalled and transport became motorized Selborne was often cut off in the winter. White's friends frequently complained about the inconvenience of visiting him at home, suggesting that he should move to Oxford or London.

* * *

Perhaps there's something to be said for staying put, for being committed to locality. Today, bombarded as we are with incessant and bewildering consumer choice, we've become experts at keeping our options open, of forever wondering 'What next?' and 'Where to, next?' and 'Who with, next?' How liberating, in a sense: the thought of choosing to stay 'here', instead, as well as resisting the urge to be available perpetually to the outside world.

Imagine switching off, for a season, to focus intently on what's in front of you, as Gilbert White managed to do so meticulously! In fact, if we were to shine the light of phenology upon our own, personal rhythms (think of a typical day, week, season or year) we might quickly spot a painful lack of time for solitude, rest, activity that feeds the soul, or even singular focus. Culturally, we seem to spend our energy, with extraverted extravagance, on doing lots of things at once. But how much care do we bring to the art of renewal?

* * *

These ancient roadways into Selborne certainly heighten the atmosphere, as they deliver us safely into the village, passing the delightfully named Gracious Street and the Whites' grandish old family home, the Wakes, which is now a museum.

We park behind the Selborne Arms, and from here walk the short distance to the base of the Hanger, a steep hillside that rises sharply over the village and is still very much draped with White's 'pendulous boughs' of beech.

* * *

The way to the top is via 'the Zig-Zag', a path composed of about 20 sharply zig-zagging sections which make the ascent up this vertiginous face of downland passable, and which Gilbert and his brother John created in 1753.

The shady banks of the Zig-Zag could otherwise be known

*as 'the Hanging Gardens of Selborne' – still flush as they
are with the remains of ferns, wild flowers and shrubs from
last summer. In a few months, this will be a wall of brightly
coloured greenery again.*

*We reach the top to behold White's 'very engaging view',
which he describes as 'an assemblage of hill, dale, wood-lands,
heath, and water'. To the north-west, on the ridge of the
Selborne Hanger, is a magnificent stand of beech trees, some
over 100 feet (30.5 m) tall. The word 'hanger' is derived from
the Old English 'hangra' meaning a steeply wooded slope,
and these trees are particularly impressive in winter with their
steely grey trunks, colossal side branches and skeletal, towering
presences.*

A stop in the go-go-go

At the top, the kind of peace that only arrives through aching
legs and a pounding heart.

We perch upon a curious antique metal bench which has
no back support, next to a Sarsen Stone that White dragged
up here (*how the ...?*), to catch our breath. The metal is cold
but we're glad of the rest, and the view inspires. You can see
the village below, like a model, with the little church we'll visit
later, which has been nestling down there for nearly 900 years.

It's good to stop, after the toil of the climb, and it strikes
us that in life and work we rarely afford ourselves the time
to pause after we accomplish anything. The urge is to keep
moving, and we need courage to go against the flow, to pause
for long enough to reflect on what we've done, or where we've
been. To enjoy the view, and to see how far we have come.

To root this physically can be ever so helpful: to choose
a bench, for example, or a favourite place to return to, as a
sacramental ritual – to say thank you, or well done to yourself,
or even just 'Wow!' for making it through. It embeds a rhythm
of gratitude and awareness, as well as placing a 'stop' within
the 'go-go-go'.

In fact, a bench is one of those few micro-spaces in our culture that affords us permission to sit and watch the world, unrushed, through our eyes and not a screen. No wonder there's something quietly soulful about them, like a presence. No wonder, too, that people love to dedicate a bench to the memory of a loved one. Aren't they memorials to all the times we ever chose to stop to love the place we're in?

Our not-so common commons

On the top of the hill is a swathe of land called Selborne Common. Commons have a fascinating history which in many ways encapsulates the struggle between agricultural workers and landowners over many centuries.

Until the seventeenth century, there were millions of acres of common land in England where local people had rights: typically to graze livestock, mow meadows for hay, gather firewood and cut turf for domestic fuel, and occasionally to extract minerals for local use or, if there was a pond or a river nearby, to fish. For poor farm labourers and their families (and most of Selborne's villagers would have been in this category during medieval and earlier times) access to the commons could make the difference between life and death, particularly during the winter.

The process of 'enclosure' – with individuals buying the exclusive ground rights and all common rights to the agricultural landscape – became more widespread during the sixteenth century, and by the nineteenth century unenclosed commons had become restricted to large areas of rough pasture in mountainous regions and to quite small residual parcels of land in the lowlands of England.

Selborne Common, then, represents a relatively rare example of common land that has survived in the south of England, a reminder of the common bond we share not just with humanity, but with the land.

The shapeliness of trees

Today, we are with our friend Michelle, a photographer, and she's fascinated by the bare trees we can see as we walk. 'It's a lovely time of year to look at trees because you can see the *shape* of them,' she reflects, with an artist's eye. It's true; we pause to admire a beech that has two trunks, giving what looks like a great Churchillian 'V for victory' to us, which is the polite way of reading it.

Contemplation doesn't have to involve some kind of super-spirituality; really, it's about the deeper connection that comes through seeing afresh. And one simple way to look more closely at the natural world is to sketch the shape of a bare tree in winter. It doesn't matter if you can't draw; the process will slow you down, and invites you to look closely, with curious eyes.

It's also fun – and fruitful – to try sketching with your 'weaker' hand – which allows the brain to process in a different, more creative and reflective way, and requires that you draw what you *see*, instead of what your mind *predicts* is there (which is what we usually do). Gilbert White was a natural observer *par excellence*, a man who was able to watch the world closely with the naked eye; for those of us who struggle to notice the detail, drawing with the weaker hand can be a *spiritual* practice, because it helps us to approach life itself (not just a bare tree in winter) with closer, non-judgemental awareness and observation; without presumption, and with care.

Further along the path, we see incredible root patterns exposed on the sheer sides of the hangers – tangled up, but hanging on. 'Like me,' reflects Michelle. Like us all, no doubt.

* * *

It won't be long before the beech leaves come out, now: dark brown candle-like buds seem poised to reveal their translucently soft, lime-green leafiness … but not quite. Now is not the time for leaf, but bud. We must wait patiently, as creation is willing to wait. A reminder to those of us who strain forwards restlessly and anxiously, that 'there is a time for everything', as the Bible puts it in Ecclesiastes (3.1).

In the meantime, there's plenty up here to distract the senses, even on this monochrome day: muted tones of crisp orangey bracken, all dishevelled like a bad hair day, and garlanded by the blooming yellow gorse. Lichen – 'Usnea', Howard informs me – hangs like bushy strands of a wizard's grey beard from the branches of shrubs and small trees. Bright green moss has tried to carpet everything else up here that can't move, and it all feels unsettlingly other-worldly, as if a set from Dr Who.

On our left, the view opens out across to Noar Hill in the distance, which was a favourite haunt of the celebrated nature poet Edward Thomas. Thomas drew inspiration from White's work when he lived in the South Country before the Great War. It is poignant to imagine White gazing from this spot across to Noar Hill, and Thomas returning the gaze, a century and a half later; and it feels as if there really is a 'kindredness', across time, and within place, through the wondering watch of people, planted.

Follow your nose!

Walking across Selborne Common on this freezing February morning feels like entering a natural war zone. In all directions, twisted fallen trees, some the victims of the winter's storms. One old beech has literally been split from top to bottom. Another giant has lost a substantial part of its main trunk, and several large side branches. It has fallen across an area of hollow ground, creating a subterranean world that we explore like divers in the hold of a sunken ship.

Nearby, an ancient oak is poised to split in a similar way but is somehow managing to hold itself together. It seems remarkable that these huge trees, with their widely spreading boughs, remain upright on a still day, let alone in a furious storm.

Fundamental to the strength of trees is an inner core of old wood. The cellulose of its cell walls is impregnated with the 'steel' of the natural world, a substance called lignin. Lignin is incredibly strong and resistant to rot. There's a subtlety and sensibility about the slow growth of trees and the various ways in which lignin can be deposited to provide extra strength for the support of the branches. Another reminder, if needed, to those of us who are impatient, that a good pace is not always about speed.

* * *

You can see right through the great crack in the oak tree. Michelle buries her face in the fissure and exclaims, 'I don't think I've ever smelled a tree before.' (Have you?) 'It's like smelling history, like the glorious smell of an old musty book that's not been opened in many years ...'

I put my nose in, and it's true, it's evocative. In fact, it takes me to church – it's like stepping into an ancient chapel, with that immediate hit of musty glory that you get when you open the door. Perhaps the next time I step into an old church, its smell will take me back to this tree, which is a much more natural way round.

The beautiful process of decay

Despite the deep frost and ice up here on the common, it's tantalizing to glimpse very early signs of spring: the emerging leaves of bluebells and wild garlic; gorse, just coming into flower in sheltered places; hazel trees glowing with catkin 'lanterns'.

From time to time, we come across what looks like, from a distance, an evergreen tree capped with a crown of dark green leaves. On closer inspection, however, these are the trunks of dead trees that are supporting massive overgrowths of ivy, which provide invaluable shelter in the winter for flocks of small birds, roosting bats, overwintering butterflies and a host of smaller insects. It's an example of the common's many microhabitats: smaller spaces within the overall ecosystem of wooded pasture that provide homes for a wide variety of plants and animals.

Another such microhabitat lies underfoot. In her book The Secret Life of Flies, *the entomologist Erica McAlister explains how flies help to recycle all sorts of things, from the carpet of dead beech leaves that we're walking on, to animal 'waste', which we are trying to avoid! She writes:*

> There is no escaping the fact that dying is an essential part of life, to clear the way for the next generation. And someone, or rather many ones, have to help with this recycling process. Flies that are detritivores, the gardeners of the countryside, have larvae that munch away the dead leaves and twigs, or feed on the subsequent decaying organic mould. These flies, along with bacteria, fungi and other invertebrates, perform the incredibly valuable role of recycling nutrients back into the environment.

The apparent lifelessness of winter on Selborne Common conceals an abundance of activity, then: the decay and recycling of organic matter, as literally millions of small and microscopic organisms go about their daily work. Despite the lack of light and the low temperatures above ground, these cleaners and recyclers continue to function just a few millimetres below the surface of leaf litter and soil; fallen branches and tree stumps; dead plants and animals; cowpats and other animal waste.

We realize just how strangely beautiful the process of decay can be, especially as we pause to look more closely at a dense cluster of small, overlapping bracket fungi on a tree stump no more than ten centimetres in diameter. It's a kaleidoscope of layered colours from almost black through deep purple, red and orange to dark blue, green, yellow and ivory; another of nature's very slow processes, happening before our eyes, but this time of breakdown, and the release of nutrients back into the environment. Each of these small spaces also represents another valuable microhabitat with its own inter-related group of living organisms.

A meditation on dung

Howard is keen to point out, with boyish joy, how one particular group of flies, the coprophages (from the Greek *copros* meaning faeces), feed specifically on animal waste. Faeces, he explains, are an excellent food source: they come in convenient packages, are already partly digested and have good nutritional value! And he shares a favourite quote from Jean Henri Fabre, the nineteenth-century French entomologist, about coprophagous flies, which helps us to sympathize: 'You think they are horrid, dirty insects; but they are not; they are busy making the world a cleaner place for you to live in.'

That's quite a reminder.

While we look down our human noses (and so often recoil) at certain creatures, they're all a crucial part of the picture. So we decide that the next time we see a fly, we'll allow it to remind us to be thankful for *all* forms of life. And there's soon an opportunity, as a fresh cowpat offers up its own unique opportunity for meditation.

A strange thing, perhaps, to behold three adults pausing reverently by such a ... deposit, but it strikes us that we try so hard to sanitize life, and yet life is happening, and goodness can be found, even and especially within the most seemingly repugnant of circumstances. It's all part of the wild whole.

A place to rest

On a similarly sobering note, graveyards are an enriching place in which to acquaint ourselves with, and even start to befriend, our own mortality; and once we've finished exploring the common, we descend the Zig-Zag, make our way through the village, and cross the road to find St Mary's Church.

The remains of the Selborne Yew, close to the church, cut a sorry sight; just the carcass of its trunk remains. White mentions it in his letters and it was reckoned to have been over 1,400 years old when it was blown over in a storm in

January 1990. Its age suggests that it was planted alongside an early Saxon chapel on the same site, or possibly even a pre-Christian, pagan place of worship.

But what a resting place this graveyard is, both for the dead and for the living; it nestles in a natural bowl, cupped lovingly, as if in the hand of God, by the steep hills that surround it. Gilbert White asked to be buried 'in as plain and private a way as possible'; and when we find his grave, tucked quietly behind the church, it is clear that his wishes were observed. The man who loved this place so much was keen to rest, without ostentation, out there in the tranquil beauty of the scene.

It is moving, standing at Gilbert's grave, to think that we return home both to God, who breathes spirit into us, *and* to the Earth, which affords us our physical birth. Both are a homecoming; both are places of rest.

I'm left here wondering, for a while, about where I would like to be buried or scattered, and what this might signify about my own sense of belonging, in life, to a place. Where would I like to be returned to? What is the place of which, in death, I would like to become most organically a part?

Your Creator loves you dearly

Despite White's modest grave, there are now two beautiful stained glass windows in the church, installed in 1920 to commemorate the 200th anniversary of his birth.

One delightfully shows the figure of St Francis of Assisi (1181–1226), surrounded on both sides by scenes of Selborne with the trees full of the different birds that have made Selborne their home. The caption underneath reads: 'Gilbert White, 1720–1793, God be praised: A humble student of nature. For a faithful priest and a writer of genius.'

St Francis, like Gilbert a long time after him, believed that nature itself was the mirror of God and that all creatures, including ourselves, should praise him. The design of this window was surely inspired by a story in the Little Flowers of St Francis, *a collection of legends about his life published towards the end of the fourteenth century. It describes Francis preaching to the birds:*

> *'My sweet little sisters, birds of the sky,' Francis said, 'you are bound to heaven, to God, your Creator. In every beat of your wings and every note of your songs, praise him. He has given you the greatest of gifts, the freedom of the air. You neither sow, nor reap, yet God provides for you the most delicious food, rivers, and lakes to quench your thirst, mountains, and valleys for your home, tall trees to build your nests, and the most beautiful clothing: a change of feathers with every season ...*
> *'Clearly, our Creator loves you dearly ...'*

Reflection on the stream: listening

I feel less self-conscious, now, about talking to the birds in my garden at home. Francis bestows upon our fellow creatures a sense of worth that in turn enriches our humanity, too. It places us back within a rhythm of soulful communion.

We leave the churchyard through a gate in the hedge at the east end and descend a steep grassy slope towards the wooded entrance to a valley. It's a timeless corner of countryside; you can't see a road and you can barely glimpse a cottage; there's just a community of ancient oaks, a few sheep, the church behind us, and the clear, fast-moving Oakhangar Stream. Another perfectly placed bench beckons, and the invitation is too lovely to resist; so we sink into a few moments of stillness there, without feeling the need to speak.

Finally, Michelle breaks the silence. 'I've only just noticed that you can hear the stream,' she whispers. She's faster than me. I hadn't yet heard it. Its burbling provides the gentlest awakening for us; it's not accusatory, but invitational. And it speaks, we decide, of the deeper flow we can find with the world when we do pause for long enough within it. It was always there; we just didn't realize it.

That doesn't have to be with a river, of course. It could be with some*one* else: present enough with them to find that deeper flow. Sometimes, that means letting each other 'be still', without filling the gaps with words – to hear that which we otherwise would have missed.

Staying the course

From here, our final challenge is to find an ancient trackway, the Via Canonorum (or 'way of the canons'), which connects Selborne village and St Mary's Church with the site of the former Selborne Priory, now Priory Farm, a mile or so along the valley.

The Via passes through Dorton Wood and there are clear signs of its antiquity: a causeway made of old cobbles and bricks, beside which a side-stream flows into the main valley; and another antiquated metal seat, set for so long against a huge old beech that its back struts are now deeply absorbed into the trunk.

We rest for a third time, and absorb the silence of this still place, even as it absorbs us.

Another few hundred yards, and we leave the wood and cross the fields to Priory Farm, thankful to have negotiated the muddiest sections without losing our boots or getting them filled with water. Due to the lack of footpath signs, we navigate the yards and gates around Priory Farm with some difficulty – it's disconcerting when you can't see the way forward! – but finally we get back on track, crossing the valley towards Coombe Wood and our return.

It is good to persevere, and we're thankful for the committed work of organizations such as the Ramblers' Association in keeping footpaths and rights of access to the countryside open. We are also mindful of the courage it takes, sometimes, to keep walking a path, literal or metaphorical, when you can't quite see where it leads.

Earth to earth

As the path brings us back towards the church, we reflect on why Gilbert White's book – so deeply rooted in one particular parish, so parochial! – has such a universal appeal.

The nature writer Robert Macfarlane surely provides us with a clue. In his book Landmarks *he proposes that our understanding of the word 'parochial' has soured over the last century by shifting in a negative way to mean something sectarian and insular. Previously, the word had a more positive meaning, to include the discovery of universal truths through knowing a place and its people well.*

Perhaps we do indeed learn best by sustained scrutiny of the close-at-hand. Certainly, his long acquaintance with Selborne helped Gilbert White to know the place 'deeply', and the continuing fascination with White's book could derive from a shared understanding that is captured by Macfarlane, who suggests that concentration within the perimeters of one particular parish results in 'knowledge cubed rather than knowledge curbed'.

My own experience has been very different from Gilbert White's. I was brought up in London but have since lived and worked at six different locations across the south of England, in small villages, towns and cities from Suffolk to Devon and from Oxfordshire to Hampshire. In Edward Thomas's words from The South Country *(written in 1909), I am one of 'those modern people who belong nowhere', and sometimes I regret it.*

* * *

I admit, I feel grateful for my own upbringing in one place in rural Kent. The little town of Cranbrook is still infused for me with a sense of home – its streets, its shops (some of which are unchanged), its people, churches, woods, playing fields, farms – I got to know them well, and loved to keep diaries about the weather and the football and cricket matches we played for the town, and our Christmas Eve walks, and regular fishing trips to the sea. Sacramental rituals performed year in, year out, with friends, grandparents, neighbours, newcomers.

The invitation to 'belong' is not, perhaps, as clear, in today's more transient culture; which makes it all the more significant to cultivate belonging, wherever we go. To see, perhaps, when the beech leaves are preparing to bud again; to find regular ways to connect with a community of people; to be part of a place, instead of simply passing through.

* * *

Back in the churchyard, we catch the scent of almond from a tree festooned in pink blossom. The air is calm, it's still light at 5pm, and the birds are in full song. Purple crocuses are offering their last uplifting splashes of colour to this unique day, nestled within snowdrops of brilliant white; a day in which we've played our own quiet and unspectacular part in the ever-unfolding sacramental drama of this place.

A shiver, not of cold but of quiet delight, breaks the surface from deep within. It could be the visceral thrill you feel, at that first moment of the year when you truly smell, or taste, or hear, or see that winter's grip on the Earth is once again weakening. The blossom does it for me, every time.

But it could, just as easily, be a soulful moment of clarity: that I am now part of this place, and this place is a part of me. Earth to earth.

A cup of tea from Howard's trusty Thermos flask restores the soul, along with a slice of cake, which we share together back at the car in the half-light. A smile between friends, and a satisfied hush. We have found our sacramental rhythm.

Activities

- Start a nature diary, where you can begin to record your first sightings, each year, of particular flowers, birds, animals and so on. Use this as a way to nurture your own personal awareness of the changing seasons, and the natural rhythms of which we are part.

- And to be more specific, why not select one tree in your locality that you can return to every month, or season (you might like to join the Woodland Trust's 'nature calendar' to help you to keep this resolution, and to support their research; visit naturescalendar.woodlandtrust.org.uk). Keep watch – and note – of when you notice the budburst, the first leaf, first ripe fruit, the first autumn tinting, full autumn tinting, leaf fall and the fully bare tree. Get to know your tree. If you're in a built-up environment, the horse chestnut is a popular 'townie' tree, and provides a really engaging display throughout the year (we will focus a little more on this particular tree in our September walk).

- Find a bench to call your own, and try to create a ritual of stopping there specifically to reflect upon, and celebrate, the completion of tasks, projects or seasons in your life.

- Sketch something in nature with your weaker hand. And keep sketching!

- Meditate on some animal excrement, or a fly.

- Sit in a graveyard and reflect upon your own mortality. Where do you feel most closely 'at home', and where would you like to be buried or scattered? It's a powerful exercise, in fact, to imagine your own funeral. Who might be there? What might they say of you? What would you like to change about the way you live now, as a result?

- Listen to the flow of a stream. Sit with it. Listen some more.

- Be willing to sit with someone in silence, without the need to fill every moment with words. Tune in to them, in a way that goes beyond words. Sense their presence, their energy, their heart.

- Return to a favourite place of yours.

- Keep watch on your own personal rhythms. Notice the ebb and flow of your energy, for instance; pay attention to how much sleep you're getting, what you're eating, how much rest you're getting, and observe what makes you come alive and feeds your soul throughout the course of a day, a week, a season, or the year.

3

March
A Wooded Corner of Hampshire

A walk within the woodland of
Great Copse, near Mottisfont

We both love Mottisfont. It's such a special place on the River Test and we often walk here. As one guidebook to the Test Way footpath explains, this is some of 'the finest country in the South, rich with wildlife and natural beauty, and rich with historical, literary and sporting associations'. And we would say 'Amen' to that!

In May, we'll explore the land around Mottisfont Abbey, managed by the National Trust. For this walk, however, we're heading past the parish church and along the country lanes from the main village, to visit one of the best examples of semi-natural ancient woodland in this part of Hampshire, Great Copse. (The epithet 'ancient' means that the wood is reckoned to be at least 400 years old.)

But a word, first, on the narrow country roads we find our-
selves walking upon. If you live in a rural parish somewhere in
England, it is likely that the roads and footpaths have been in
regular use back to medieval times and probably far beyond.
So we're conscious, as we set out for the woods, that we are
walking in the footsteps of all sorts of different people who
have travelled these ways before us ...

* * *

Simply the act of walking along a lane like this can help us to
step into a place more meaningfully. It's never quite the same
in a car; you don't smell the hedges, or hear the birds, or sense
the atmosphere ... but on foot, life is no longer a blur; with
every step you find yourself grounded, physically, spiritually,
soulfully.

The quiet country road we're walking this morning, for half
a mile or so up and out of the village towards Great Copse,
provides the opportunity for us to become present – as well
as to *present* ourselves – to the place; to honour it with our
awareness and open-hearted presence.

So we slow our pace, take some deeper breaths, and remember that we are, in a sense, pilgrims. Every walk can be a
pilgrimage: your destination doesn't need to be religious. Just
bring yourself with humility to the heart of a time or place, and
we believe you'll find God waiting there.

It's not about what we can *get* from today, but how we can
give ourselves to it, to the possibilities of our time together,
as well as to the patch of woodland we're about to explore.
And in the process, we hope to discover something more of the
soulful nature, not just of the woods, but of our selves.

* * *

There are several venerable yews and oaks in the hedges
bordering these country lanes and both trees are well known
as 'markers', planted at places of significance for the local com-
munity. 'Gospel Oaks' still mark some parish boundaries; the

Bible would have been read beneath them at Rogation-tide (in May, just before Ascension Day), when 'the bounds' were 'beaten' along the parish boundaries, as a ritual act of prayer and supplication by parishioners for a successful harvest.

The geographer Paul Hindle, writing about medieval roads and tracks, suggests that they would have been used by both lay and religious travellers – from farm workers, minstrels, messengers, merchants and outlaws, to priests, friars, pardoners and pilgrims. Even kings and queens in former times were regularly on the move along such paths, to try to keep their rebellious subjects under control.

When the Romans left Britain, the Saxons began to establish communities across the country, building churches as they went (the later Norman churches we often see today were usually built upon the site of these original Saxon buildings).

Mottisfont had a Saxon 'minster' or 'mother church', and from there priests or lay ministers would head out to six nearby villages to lead services in their smaller chapels, as there was a shortage of priests and bishops in early Anglo-Saxon times (in the fifth, sixth and seventh centuries).

In Great Copse, the woodland paths head in the direction of the scattered villages of East and West Tytherley, and Broughton, which we know, from the Domesday Book, were chapels associated with the mother church at Mottisfont. We can be confident, therefore, that priests would have been walking these very footpaths. And this would have been mirrored across the country.

Sensing our way in: from a tangle to a harmony

There is a certain kind of magic involved in entering any woodland or forest. As the Wilderness Society puts it, 'There is no wifi in the forest but you will find a better connection.' It's so true!

It's not always a perfectly serene connection, however. There is an unruly tangle of natural life and decay upon the woodland floor as we edge through the kissing gate – from broken branches, brambles and fungi, to bracken and the leaves of early woodland flowers – and the spirituality writer Eckhart Tolle suggests that this kind of sight can subtly trouble our minds (especially if we prefer our lawns and gardens neatly manicured). We like to order the world around us, and to categorize the decay (in this case) as bad, and the new growth as good ... yet it's impossible to untangle the two.

Tolle suggests a simple exercise that can help us to reconcile this sensory dissonance in a positive and helpful way. Pause, he says, to be present to the whole lot without trying to put labels upon any of it – and you can begin to see the troubling tangle as more of a *harmony*, instead. Be still, and alert, he advises:

> As soon as you sense that hidden harmony, that sacredness, you realise you are not separate from it, and when you realise that, you become a conscious participant in it. In this way, nature can help you become realigned with the wholeness of life.

* * *

That word 'wholeness' is significant, when it comes to our relationship with the natural world.

In fact, the Hebrew word found in the Bible for soul – *nephesh* – really means 'the *whole* of your being'. Usually, in day-to-day life, we operate from only a part of our being, pushed ever onwards by the restlessly insecure, judgemental chatter of the mind (which we might also call the ego). When we step back into the harmony of surroundings like this woodland, we can encounter something more of our own hidden wholeness, as we find ourselves within the greater harmony of creation itself. Wholeness doesn't come through isolation, but in relation to the whole.

So Howard and I stand still, and we let the woodland floor begin its work on us, and in us.

The soul-stirring sight of a butterfly

Before long, we are gifted with an extraordinarily happy bonus sighting; an addition to the harmony. Pausing close to the elephantine bark of a dear old yew, there's a flash of yellow and – *oh my!* – our first sighting of a brimstone butterfly this year. My immediate reaction is to punch the air with sheer delight, with wonder, with joy. Spring *is* coming!

The brimstone overwinters here, and tends to emerge in February or early March on a sunny day. And here it is, perhaps the most palpable sign yet of the new season's imminence. It is a herald.

It's a beautiful juxtaposition, too, of the monumental and the fragile; the fleeting waft of a fragile butterfly and the gnarled greatness of a tree that has made it through so many winters.

The nature writer Michael McCarthy shares our joy at such a sight. 'I have struggled,' he writes, 'to find a way of expressing my elation at seeing the first butterfly of the year. It was a bright yellow brimstone.' He continues:

> Using science, and rationality, I can tell you quite a lot about it: that it was an insect; that it belonged to the butterfly family *Pieridae*, the whites ... that in its caterpillar stage it had fed on the plants buckthorn or alder buckthorn; and that it had hibernated disguised as a leaf, probably in ivy, until the first warm day in March woke it up ...

But that doesn't *really* describe it, he says. That brimstone 'electrified me instantly':

> [I]t was the sign of the turning year, not just of the warm times coming again but of *the great rebirth of everything*, the great unstoppable renewal – and the brilliance of its colour seemed to proclaim the magnitude of the change it was signalling ...

Just one small butterfly, expressing with immeasurable eloquence the universal promise of spring; a work of art, of truth, of presence.

* * *

The visceral excitement of the sight of that brimstone serves to heighten our anticipation: what else might we see as we look into the hidden depths of the leafless trees, and how will this woodland inform us that spring is now truly on the way?

The leaves of the early flowers are already clear to see: wood violets, primroses and bluebells among them. Later in the year they will be joined by some of the classic indicators of ancient woodland: graceful Solomon's seal, bright green wood spurge and the intriguingly named herb-Paris (or true lover's knot), an unusual member of the lily family.

We notice the fresh green leaves, too, on early starters such as honeysuckle and blackthorn, and we look up into the trees again, searching for buds bursting open. Still not quite yet, they seem to say – it was a particularly cold February – but it won't be long now ...

As we continue onwards, quietly (and to state the obvious, it pays to walk quietly in the woods sometimes), we hear the drilling of a woodpecker as it excavates a new nest hole in a dead branch further away in the wood.

Oak is the dominant tree in Great Copse, with substantial numbers of hazel and a scattering of ash, hornbeam, sweet chestnut, birch and sycamore. A few conifers and yews, plus a good number of holly bushes, make up the population of evergreens.

Each tree can become a world of its own, sustaining communities that are part of the greater 'wholeness' that we are finding ourselves part of today. Spiders will be hiding in the crevices of bark, while branches themselves are draped with epiphytic ferns, mosses and lichens with their own mini-communities of invertebrates. And then of course there are the birds and the mammals: bats roosting higher up and shrews, voles and wood mice in the holes near the ground.

All of which means that when you chop down a tree, you are destroying so much more than 'just' a tree. Of course, it's also taken a long time to get there. You can't replace a 200-year-old beech tree overnight using human technology. You cannot instantly recreate a woodland. It can take centuries to re-establish a woodland fully – we're talking about cycles that are so much longer than the ones we are used to, within our world of instant gratification. This is sobering when you consider that, according to the BBC News, an area the size of a football pitch is cleared in the Amazon rainforest every minute.

So it's a profoundly important notion to respect how long this particular woodland might have taken to get here. In fact, the footprint of this wood probably goes back thousands of years, and there are huge consequences to destroying it.

* * *

I'm reminded of a couple of inspiring stories, the first about New College, Oxford. When it was founded and built in 1379, huge oak timbers were used to hold up the roof of its great dining hall.

Legend has it that in order to provide replacement timbers for the roof's eventual repair, the college foresters planted a grove of oaks on college land. In the end, the timbers needed replacing in the 1800s, by which time the planted oaks, at 500 years old or so, were great enough to supply timber for the new roof.

The fire at Notre-Dame cathedral in Paris destroyed a roof made of timber from 'primary' forests, whose wood was probably 400 years old when the roof was constructed 900 years ago. Sadly, due to the human impact on ancient forests in northern Europe, France has no trees large enough, today, to replace those timbers like-for-like.

It takes both foresight and humility to plant ahead for something that will not grow to maturity within our own lifetimes. Dare we think beyond ourselves?

* * *

And certainly, when it comes to the natural world and the climate emergency, it's time to do just that – to think in terms of the future, while learning to live accordingly, sacrificially and sustainably now.

It can often feel as if there's very little we can do, personally, in the face of de-forestation, for example, or the great extinction of species, yet a second story, of the inspirational Jadav Payeng, might bring some added hope.

He is also known as 'the forest man of India', and lives in Majuli, the world's largest river island, which is home to over 150,000 people. During the monsoons, the river floods and erodes the soil, and since 1917 the island has lost more than half its land-mass. In fact, the rate of erosion is now accelerating so fast that scientists fear most of the island could be gone in twenty years.

Jadav Payeng decided he wanted to do something about it. But what can one person do? He went to his village elders and asked for assistance, perhaps to plant some trees where soil had been washed away; they laughed at him, but gave him 20 bamboo shoots, anyway. So he built a fence, cultivated the bamboo, and began collecting seeds from other trees, too, which he planted, one at a time, day by day, in an area of completely barren land.

He started in 1979, and now, 40 years later, through thousands of small, faithful acts of planting, he has a growing forest which covers more than 550 hectares. Stunningly, it has also become shelter to a vivid array of wildlife, including 115 elephants which live there for three months of the year. The ecosystem also supports rhino, deer and five Bengal tigers, as well as vultures, which have returned to the area after many years.

And all of this, because one man planted one tree at a time, single-handedly. Whatever our own 'tree' might represent today – a lifestyle change, perhaps? – we can surely plant one. And after that, we can plant the next ...

The bad birdwatchers' guide

Sauntering further in, a stillness hangs over (or is it within?) the woods that feels less of a silence than a presence. Whether it's the presence of the trees growing at the pace of – what, wisdom? – or the creatures ghosting around unseen, or the past, or God, I'm not entirely sure; there's no reason why it's not all of those, and more, of course.

But one thing you begin to notice, within that still presence, is the birdsong. It's stirring. But I realize, in a moment of unexpected frustration, that I'm still not very good at recognizing even the simplest of songs!

Mercifully, the journalist and ornithologist Simon Barnes – in an encouraging book called *How to be a Bad Birdwatcher: To the Greater Glory of Life* – tells us not to worry if we can't identify everything we see or hear, so long as we pause to notice that it's *there*.

Barnes' own epiphany arrived when he stood watching house-martins flying above a London cemetery. He had been hurrying to catch a train but had seen the birds and felt compelled to stop and look, despite not knowing what they were. As he watched, a bird of prey – a hobby, as he later discovered – swooped out of the blue, lightning-fast, and attacked the martins.

It was a raw and amazing sight and an exceptional moment for him, which filled him with shock and wonder. And this taught him a lesson: 'Before understanding comes the wonder, comes the delight,' he reflects. 'And that is the first aim of being a bad birdwatcher: the calm delight of the utterly normal, and the rare and sudden delight of the utterly unexpected.'

Gorgeous. A few blue tits flit by, pausing for a micro-second or two on the green sheen of a beech trunk, before continuing their purposeful passage through the woods. I know what *they* are. But the prospect of taking calm delight in them frees me from craving anything rarer, or more sensational, or even 'spiritual', for the sake of it.

'The only real skill involved in this perfect birdwatching moment,' reflects Simon Barnes, with hindsight, 'was the willingness to look.'

Kneeling for a closer look

The woodland floor is worth a closer look, too, especially after the winter storms we've just experienced, which have torn rotten branches from the tree-tops and scattered them everywhere. These branches are often covered with an array of colourful lichens.

We sink watchfully (and reverentially) to our knees to observe some moss that is growing upon the bark of a rotting tree trunk. I'm glad to have brought a magnifying lens which gives us a close-up view of the incredible fruiting structure of moss.

This exquisite piece of natural design comprises a short brown stalk, like a fine thread of hair, which protrudes upwards out of the green for about an inch (2–3 cm). At its tip is a little structure called a capsule, which contains the moss spores. And at the end of the capsule there's an exit, a bit like a poppy seed case.

The exit on a moss stalk has two sets of overlapping 'peristome' teeth which are hygroscopic: that is, they move, depending on the amount of water in them. When the air is moist and likely to be rainy, they close tight. As the weather dries out and conditions are better for releasing spores, the teeth bend open. The peristome on the end of the stalk is only about half a millimetre across, yet its structure perfectly fits its function.

* * *

Unexpected delight. Howard's simple magnifying glass, combined with his knowledge, has enabled me to see something I have literally never seen before in my life. The fruiting structure is a gorgeous burnt-orange colour with that amazing tip to it, and you can even see the spores through the translucent pod. It's a humbling example of the microscopic, the kind of precise and breath-taking details that have always been there, right before our eyes, but to which we would normally be oblivious.

We are touched again by the capacity to wonder. Sometimes

it's easy to think we've seen it all, and even if we haven't, we can Google it. And yet, stretched out on the floor of this woodland, with dampness seeping into the knees, my eyes have been opened.

* * *

The poet, priest and philosopher John O'Donohue writes, 'What you encounter, recognize or discover depends to a large degree on the *quality* of your approach ... When we approach with reverence, great things decide to approach us.'

There are any number of things in life that we could approach differently, from moment to moment – with reverence, instead of, say, with judgement or over-familiarity. The dawning of this one unique day. The simple gifts we've already been given. The presence of God, within them.

I'm humbled by the microscopic care of the Creator, and realize that I'm still in danger of seeing God more as some kind of capricious genie than as the life-giving presence within an exquisitely delicate, infinitesimally small and yet infinitely expansive universe of matter and spirit.

* * *

At the far end of the wood, we descend into what feels like a secret valley; at least, you'll only find it if you're prepared to walk for a few miles. A glassy stream winds its way through the trees along a gravelly bed. Beyond it, a few unusually small fields are bounded by thick hedges, and in the distance there's more woodland. Behind us stands a coppiced area of hazel.

A deep sense of history and continuity pervades. We imagine a Saxon peasant wandering along this path gathering firewood, or a medieval farmer passing by with his pigs, foraging hungrily for acorns and beech nuts.

As we pause by the stream, it strikes us that this flow, too, is an ancient form of 'pathway'. It has probably followed this course for hundreds if not thousands of years, fed by a nearby spring. In fact, though we don't know the name of this particular little tributary of the River Test, the names of water-ways are often the oldest names we speak, frequently flowing all the way back to the Celts.

Celtic syllables such as 'ach', 'dur', 'ex' and 'lin' are often preserved in the names of rivers and streams today. 'Ach' is pronounced 'ash', for example, and speaks of water; the principal source of the River Test, a spring that rises through the chalk 20 miles or so north-east of here, is close by the village of Ashe. Happily, our streams and rivers continue to murmur the words, the culture, the still-living human connection to Earth of those who came long, long before us.

The tributary itself is like a small vein running towards the artery of the Test. I'm not sure if we think of rivers and streams as being alive, but just as blood means life to a body, so, surely, does water to the Earth. And so, it's fair to say that this unremarkable stream *is* anciently alive; in a sense, it's the life behind the life.

In Mary Oliver's poem 'At the River Clarion', the nature poet sits beside a river all afternoon, listening to it. And it's only after a long time of listening that she discerns what it's saying. 'Said the river I am part of holiness,' she writes. She's not saying that the river is God, necessarily. But God flows through the river.

It's reason enough to rest upon a fallen tree, its moss like a cushion; to pull out the flask, and to sense the connection. Another poet is evoked, this time Rilke: 'being here is so much'.

Pheasants stroll the field beyond the stream, heads forward, tails back like pointer dogs; buzzards patrol above them, with enviable nonchalance, while a collection of sheep have spaced themselves out across the fields as if posing for a painting. These, too, are part of holiness. Holiness seems to flow here, like water.

How to tell an old hedge

After our time of stillness, our attention is drawn to the hedges around the small fields opposite. Brian has wondered if this unusual field pattern suggests that this, too, is an ancient scene.

There's a way of telling. Cultivated land was originally demarcated and divided by digging boundary ditches or planting hedges. An old hedge will usually be deep and contain a wide variety of woody plants, ranging from towering ash and sycamore trees to smaller hawthorn and maple and less conspicuous climbers like honeysuckle and clematis. In the 1960s, the naturalist M. D. Hooper and his associates investigated many kilometres of old hedgerow in several English counties using Anglo-Saxon land charters to locate them. Hooper came up with a 'ready reckoner' to calculate the age of a hedge: in every 30 metres of hedgerow, each different woody species counts for about 100 years. For example, if a survey reveals at least eight different woody species consistently along several 30-metre sections of hedgerow, it is about 800 years old.

Of course, many factors determine which woody plants succeed in establishing themselves in a particular hedgerow and so Hooper's calculator is certainly not a 'law' of nature. However, it is reasonable to assume that if a hedge has a good variety of well-established woody plants it is old – indeed, like these hedges before us! – and may well date back to Saxon times.

Old hedges are as much a haven for wildlife as ancient woodlands, and it is a cause of regret that so many have been removed since World War Two to make fields larger and more easily cultivated with modern machinery.

Old wounds, fresh wisdom

As we begin to head back, we are moved by looking upwards into an old tree, whose dead, lightning-struck branches are a reminder of past damage, as are the cankers on the trunk. Swollen, circular areas of bark indicate where branches have been torn off and the healing processes of the tree have gradually repaired the wound. Comfortingly, we can see, from the buds, that despite their damage these scarred old trees are very much alive and will be yielding new leaves in the spring. They can be a powerful metaphor for the time and patience needed for the healing of past hurts, and I've found that just spending time with them can help to nurture such patience.

Old trees have a broad and deep 'rootedness', too. Perhaps one advantage of the later stages of life (there must be some!) is that greater insight may come from broader experience combined with deeper understanding ... that, and, hopefully, the humility to admit that there's more we don't know now than when we started out!

To pay our last respects to winter, we turn over a rotten log and watch much crawling and scurrying as worms, beetles, centipedes and an assortment of other many-legged creatures hurry back into the darkness of the leaf litter.

A hidden harmony

Those broken branches, and this rotten log, induce a poignant sense of introspection in us both. Howard's mention of paying our last respects to winter strikes a chord; usually we're so keen to see the back of the season that we neglect what it might have taught us. A time for dormancy and rest, a stripping back of the superfluous, of the sense of clarity and focus that comes with it, and even that mysterious beauty of decay.

Perhaps, by thanking winter, it will be a little easier to welcome its arrival next year. I'm grateful for the biting cold days we've had, for childlike fun in glistening snow, for the comforting glow of fire-pits and marshmallows, for star-gazing in the dark evenings; for all the celebrations – fireworks, Christmas, New Year – and for the fresh start that winter always seems to offer us, as it clears the decks and resets the clock.

As we watch the fomenting bugs subside and fade back into the shelter of pine needles and crispy leaves, we circle back to the idea of life and decay intertwined – that sacred harmony of which Eckhart Tolle writes.

Howard speaks very personally about his own mortality, as we wander past another great piece of wood that has fallen, clearly a long time ago, and is now so decayed that it is embedded in earth and leaf and mulch, part of the woodland floor. 'We won't be fully human if we don't yield to the passing of the seasons in our own lives,' he says. What a prospect: that we can become more fully 'who we are' through the very process of disintegration.

There is a mysterious beauty to this, waiting to be discovered where we might least expect it. Here in March, we are now well into the spiritual season of Lent, in which we 'deny' ourselves (by giving something up, or by fasting, for instance) in order to remember the time when Jesus faced down temptation in the desert, and to prepare for Easter. The poet Jean Watt writes of a different way of seeing through the trees, *before* the new life, and new growth, really begins again. There is beauty *here*.

> Lent is a tree without blossom, without leaf,
> Barer than blackthorn in its winter sleep,
> All unadorned. Unlike Christmas which decrees
> The setting-up, the dressing-up of trees,
> Lent is a taking down, a stripping bare,
> A starkness after all has been withdrawn
> Of surplus and superfluous,
> Leaving no hiding-place, only an emptiness
> Between black branches, a most precious space
> Before the leaf, before the time of flowers;
> Lest we should see only the leaf, the flower,
> Lest we should miss the stars.

* * *

It will soon be the spring equinox, too, that time of equal day and night, which reminds us that light and dark do not have to be in competition with, or in opposition to, each other; but in harmony.

At a parish church called Holy Trinity in Barsham, Suffolk, every year, precisely on the spring and autumn equinox, the setting sun (if it's not cloudy!) pours through a narrow fourteenth-century window in the church tower, to illuminate a five-foot-high carving of Jesus in the centre of the nave, for four magical minutes.

It's perhaps made all the more special because this intriguing spectacle was lost for several centuries. The carving of Jesus stands on top of the rood screen, but it was torn down during the Reformation in the 1500s. Happily, it was rebuilt in 1870 with an identical figure of Jesus in exactly the same position – but the *window*, meanwhile, was blocked when the vicar at the time hung a painting over it (he wasn't to know, of course)!

After a fire in 1979, the picture was taken down, so finally the scene was set. But it was still another few years before a curate at the church, John Buchanan, was present enough to witness the equinoctial illumination, and to realize that it happened by design, not accident. He told a local newspaper,

It is just incredible to see this brilliant shaft of sunlight illuminate Christ on the Cross. It is a magical moment ... The church is in gloom, as it is dusk, and then all of a sudden the setting sun is in exactly the right position to shine this brilliant beam of light through the window.

Whatever the reasons in the 1300s for engineering this twice-yearly event, there's something truly poignant about those dying rays of light illuminating Jesus on the cross. The equinox is, after all, a moment of supreme poise, in which we all share an equal measure of day and night, across the world.

And, on the Cross, Christians believe that Jesus holds so many seemingly opposite things, so many potentially irreconcilable things, together within the moment: light and dark, the inner world and the outer, the 'spiritual' and the physical, the particular and the universal, the divine and the human, death and life itself.

'In him,' writes the apostle Paul, 'all things hold together' (Colossians 1.17).

And thus, when it feels to us that it's all too much, and we're no longer able to hold it all together – the good news is that we, too, are held.

* * *

We are almost back at the entrance to the wood. A contented stillness has settled between us, and within us. We are where we are. And soul calls to soul in a place such as this, although rarely in words.

Another brimstone floats past, right on cue. We punch the air, silently.

Sweet harmony.

Activities

- Find a tangled woodland floor, and allow yourself to meditate upon its harmony. Spend as long as you need with it! Feel part of a greater wholeness, and reflect, too, on anything in your own life that feels like a tangle of 'good' and 'bad'. How might you better see this as a natural harmony?
- Take a hand-lens or magnifying glass to the woods, and look closely at a sample of moss.
- See what kind of life you can find and identify around a rotting piece of dead wood, or as you peel away bark from a fallen branch. Spend some time reflecting on what you've had to let go of, and on the nature of your own mortality.
- Do some bird-watching. Enjoy the calm delight of the utterly normal, and keep watch, too, for the rare and sudden delight of the utterly unexpected.
- Plant a tree. Use this as a way of reflecting on how you view the longer term, the world beyond yourself. What can you do, today, that will have a positive impact on future generations?

- Identify an old hedge, and try to estimate its age by counting the number of different woody species you can see in a 30-metre stretch.
- Sit with a stream or within a wood and sense the holiness of creation. Be aware of the holiness that flows within you. What difference does it make to life, if you are able to see creation, and yourself within it, as 'part of holiness'?
- Say goodbye to winter well. Reflect or journal on all the blessings of the season, as well as the challenges. What have you learned, this winter? What has been stripped back? What can you actively welcome about the coming of next winter? Write yourself a note – which you can read as winter approaches, next year!
- Step outside and look for the beauty of starlight between the bare branches of a tree. Use this as a way to meditate upon the unusual beauty you find in unexpected places of your life; in the places or times or seasons in which things have been stripped bare, perhaps.

4

April
In Pursuit of Spring

*A walk at Steep, Hampshire, in the footsteps
of the poet Edward Thomas*

The sun had both dried the turf and warmed it. By the side
of the road were the first bluebells and cowslips. They were
not growing there, but some child had gathered them ... and
then, getting tired of them, had dropped them. They were
beginning to wilt, but they lay upon the grave of Winter. I was
quite sure of that. Winter may rise up through mould alive
with violets and primroses and daffodils, but when cowslips
and bluebells have grown over his grave he cannot rise again:
he is dead and rotten, and from his ashes the blossoms are
springing. Therefore, I was very glad to see them.
(Edward Thomas, *In Pursuit of Spring*)

*It's one of those days when it feels good to be alive! The welcome
sunlight has a greater intensity after the recent grey weather.*

We're gathered with a small group of walkers at the Church of All Saints, in Steep – a village just north of Petersfield in Hampshire. Our plan today is to follow in the footsteps of the author and poet Edward Thomas (1878–1917), who was a keenly observant naturalist. He lived here in Steep for much of his short life, before he was killed at Arras during World War One.

Robert Macfarlane, in the introduction to one of Thomas's most beloved prose books, The South Country, *records poignant memories from the poet's wife:*

> *'His greatest pleasure, and certainly his greatest need, was to walk and be alone,' remembered his widow, Helen. Sometimes he carried a map with him, wanting to tramp for a day 'without touching a road but to cross it'. More often, he preferred to go mapless, and follow the leads of the landscape – to 'trace a stream up to its source in the wood', or to be 'guided by the hills or the sun'.*

Sacred space

Today, we have a map – in fact, we're following a circular walk that will take in Thomas's various residences in this area, and some of the sublime countryside that kept him company.

We also have a well-thumbed copy of his *Collected Poems* to refer to – another map, of sorts. Thomas left around 140 poems in a two-year burst of creativity at the end of his short life, but with it he left us this local area, too – still remarkably unspoilt – which he explored and expressed through his poetry.

First, however, we choose to pause with our group of six, to ensure that we begin well. And the little church is a fitting place to do just that. Its stones seem to have absorbed so many years of atmosphere. The late-morning light lands softly in pools upon the pillars of its Norman arches, just as it would have done in the poet's day.

I'm reminded of the tree that smelled like a church when we were in Selborne. Don't the inside and the outside of our lives all form part of the same holy space?

There is really no separation between a stone sanctuary and the natural vaults of tree and sky that we are set to explore. That said, this set-aside space does whisper of all the human rites it has tended carefully – of the baptisms, weddings and funerals; of the ever-circling rhythm of Advent, Christmas, Lent, Easter, Pentecost; of the myriad ordinary days in between, when people have come to this place, lifted the latch, hushed their voices and stepped within.

The air feels charged with the presence of people and God. We fan out to different corners of the church, to share and to yield to its gentleness; offering ourselves to this unique moment, set within a vast continuum of worship.

Windows upon Thomas and the natural world

The church has a pair of small but captivating windows in memory of Edward Thomas, which whet our appetite for our walk. Originally designed and engraved by Laurence Whistler, they were dedicated by the poet R. S. Thomas in 1978, the centenary of Edward Thomas's birth.

One window has an etching of a green road across the hills that the poet loved to follow on his solitary travels. The road is bordered by old yew trees and blossoming hawthorn. Thomas's jacket hangs on a branch, together with his pipe and walking stick, as if they're awaiting his return.

The other window is engraved with one of his poems and, high above it, just discernible in the mist, is the Red House (also known as the New House). This was one of three homes in which Thomas and his family lived at different times during their years at Steep, located on the edge of the North Downs' escarpment with spectacular views to the south. This window also depicts a sequence of doors, some shut, others open; the final one opens on to a Flanders battlefield ... Thomas's story, like the window, is scored with pathos.

When it's time for us to step back through our own door, into the light, we make for Northfield Wood, just across the road from the church. Several orange-tip butterflies are enjoying the sunshine, flitting along the woodland border and searching for their main food plants, garlic mustard and lady's smock (or cuckooflower). The path down through the coppiced hazel is steep and muddy, after all the winter's snow and rain, but it's exhilarating to see the first bluebells coming into flower.

* * *

As a child, Thomas was inspired in particular by Gilbert White and the nature writer Richard Jeffries (whom we'll discover in August); he had an eye, and a love, for nature that would rival theirs. He described himself simply as 'an inhabitant of the Earth', and though he was tormented with intellectual self-doubt and suffered bouts of crippling depression, there was something about stepping into the countryside that reconnected him with a sense of the transcendent.

In his 1914 prose work *In Pursuit of Spring* (a delightful account of his walking and cycling west, one Easter, to meet spring as it headed east), he describes an experience in woodland after a huge downpour, in which the birdsong sounds to him as he imagines it would have done upon the first day of creation; and he responds:

> As I went along I found myself repeating with an inexplicable fervour the words, 'Glory be to the Father, and to the Son, and to the Holy Ghost, as it was in the beginning, is now, and ever shall be, world without end, Amen.' No possible supplication ... could have been more satisfying.

Thomas wrestled with the notion of belief, and was certainly not at all a natural Christian, which makes his spontaneous response that much more moving. It seemed to him to require no further explanation, or justification.

So as we watch the orange-tips and savour the bluebells, we permit ourselves to speak those words quietly and simply aloud as a group together:

Glory be to the Father,
and to the Son,
and to the Holy Ghost ...
As it was in the beginning,
is now,
and ever shall be,
world without end,
Amen.

And as one of our group observes, those words 'seem to come alive in a whole new way, within the sanctuary of woodland'.

* * *

In her wonderful little book about prayer called *Help, Thanks, Wow* Anne Lamott writes: 'When Sam was six or so, he explained to me why we call God "God": "Because when you see something so great, you just go, '*God!*'"'

It doesn't have to be blasphemous. And if you can't quite go there, then 'wow!' is an appropriate response, too. 'Wow,' she writes, 'because you are almost speechless, but not quite. You can manage, barely, this one syllable. That's a *prayer*.'

And it's a prayer that expresses, even precipitates, a sense of movement, when we do step into the flow of wonder, gratitude, response. Wow has a 'reverberation', she says: '*wowowowowow*'. It's like a pulse that can soften us, just as the current that pulses through the electrodes used by a chiropractor or physiotherapist can relax our cramped muscles. 'The movement of grace from hard to soft, distracted to awake, mean to gentle again, is mysterious but essential.'

* * *

We exit the wood in the valley bottom and pause to take in delightful views towards the chalk escarpment of the North Downs and our eventual destination, the beech woods of Ashford Hanger, less than a mile away. Looking across the landscape, the emerging leaves on the trees give the impression of at least 50 shades of green. It's an amazing monochrome palette, ranging from the very palest of the newly emerging beech leaves to the darkest, almost black, of the scattered yews.

The steep, narrow lane we're on through the hamlets of Little Langleys and Ashford Chace is certainly a very old road to the Downs. Over the centuries, just as at Selborne, it has been eroded by the feet and the wheels of people, livestock, carts and carriages to the point where the surface is now 20 feet (6 m) or more below the level of the surrounding fields.

The fact that Thomas walked these lanes adds another layer of depth to them, especially as we know that his journey would lead him ultimately away to the war, never to return. He connected nature and humanity profoundly, seeing our own transience, beauty and sorrow within the shifting seasons. His poem 'In Memoriam', written in April 1915, evokes poignantly our relationship with the Earth, and the season:

The flowers left thick at nightfall in the wood
This Eastertide call into mind the men,
Now far from home, who, with their sweethearts, should
Have gathered them and will do never again.

Alongside the road are ancient yews and oaks, several of them covered in ivy and towering high above us, their roots half-exposed like veins in the steep roadside banks. Between the trees, narrow fox and badger tracks indicate that, after dark, these quiet lanes are haunted by wildlife. It is a gloomy, secret place and feels cold even though we are sheltered here and enjoying a sunny, spring day.

In pursuit of the source

Thomas loved to trace a stream or river up to its source, and we have an opportunity to do the same, as we turn left on to a footpath that takes us into Ashford Hangers National Nature Reserve, and up through the narrow valley of Lutcombe Bottom.

It's like stepping into another world: the valley, known as a combe, is roofed with towering beech trees. Thomas described it as 'ever dark, ancient and dark'. We walk just a hundred yards or so up and in, alongside a fast-flowing stream, to discover a wide, inviting pool of clear water that offers an atmospheric place to catch breath.

This is Lutcombe Pond, fed from a little further upstream by a spring. We're going to continue up the valley to search for it, but before we do, we reflect together on the words of the Catholic priest Raimon Panikkar: 'I am one with the source insofar as I act as a source by making everything I have received flow again.'

It's tempting to store things up in life; to dam the stream, if you like, for the sake of our own security and benefit. Yet there's a different way of being, a way of 'flow' to discover, if we are willing.

One way to find it is to start by giving thanks for what we have already received. So that's what we do. Beside this pond, we give thanks quietly in our own hearts.

It's wonderful what flows once you begin. My own thoughts turn to those who have helped me, with encouragement, advice, practical support, hospitality, a listening ear, a friendly smile. So much has come towards me, I can see. But what have I passed on, from them, to others? And what have I prevented from flowing through me, for fear that I would lose out by letting it go?

* * *

It's curious how powerful a practice this kind of reflection is, when you try it outside. You quickly add nature to the list, too.

It's made all the more compelling as we head up the valley, and the feeder stream becomes narrower and narrower until it seems almost to disappear. We scramble 20 feet (6 m) or so further down the steepish banks of the valley into some scrub, and ... *there*! We can now see the spring.

Standing here in quiet reverence once more, with a source of water that is gushing miraculously from below an unremarkable collection of rocks, we ask to be made one with the Source, and to let that Source flow through us.

Onwards and upwards

The woodland floor in all directions burgeons with wild garlic, its strong scent filling the air, and among the garlic a carpet of ferns, flowering dog's mercury, ghostly-white wood anemones and bright green wood spurge. Overhead a tracery of delicate young beech leaves completes the feeling that we are being literally embraced by the exhilarating freshness of spring.

As we move on, we take a steepling old trackway which leads us up towards the top of Lutcombe Bottom. Thomas walked this regularly. We're reminded of Gilbert White climbing the Zig-Zag path to Selborne Hanger just a few miles north of us. The sides of the valley here are covered with dense woodland. Under our feet are deep layers of decaying leaves from previous winters, plus an abundance of moss-covered dead wood that ranges in size from finely divided twigs to massive whole trees, victims of disease or storms.

* * *

This is one of the most deliciously untouched and evocative places I have ever seen. Thomas wrote of the walk up here in his poem 'The Path', and we pause to read it now, noticing his poet's eye for the mosses we can see, which back in his day, too, tried 'to cover roots and crumbling chalk/With gold, olive, and emerald'. There is nothing to see, he says, but,

> ... the road, the wood that overhangs
> And underyawns it, and the path that looks
> As if it led on to some legendary
> Or fancied place where men have wished to go
> And stay; till, sudden, it ends where the wood ends.

And it's so true! While you're on the path, it feels as if you're being taken mystically somewhere beyond your own knowing. Perhaps the secret is to let it draw you there, while you are on it; to let your imagination reconnect with a hidden place within you.

For yes, the path does, then, suddenly end, and you are upon the road. And though it feels as if this journey could have continued on and on, hypnotically, we find ourselves instead on Cockshott Lane, lungs bursting, hearts pumping, thankfulness overflowing, before we head east along the top of the ridge.

Arts and crafts

A short distance along Cockshott Lane we find a cluster of buildings, including several open-sided barns containing neatly stacked piles of hardwood planks. This is the Edward Barnsley Workshop, founded in 1923 by one of the most important British furniture makers of the twentieth century. Barnsley was a leading figure in the Arts and Crafts movement, a creative response to the perceived decline in standards of design and manufacture associated with mass production.

The workshop, still making fine furniture by hand, has four young apprentices who are learning the traditional skills of cabinet making. We pause outside for a chat, to exchange thoughts about the beauty of objects made from wood and the inspiration for their design that so often comes from the natural world.

It's a happy reminder of our human capacity – and calling? – to create, to hone, to fashion, to craft with our hands, to make things soulfully, simply, expertly, beautifully. We're left wondering, too, what we possess that is not plastic, disposable and consumerist, but that has been made, with loving care, to last.

* * *

Just beyond Barnsley's workshop, the shady verge of the lane is enhanced by a work of divine craft, in the form of several delicate fritillaries. These distinctive plants are increasingly rare in the wild but their purple, pink and white flowers nodding in the wind can provide a wonderful accompaniment to spring, particularly in damp meadows that have not been sprayed with herbicides.

On the opposite side of the lane stands the Arts-and-Crafts-influenced 'Red House', designed and built for Edward Thomas by his friend (and the original owner of the furniture work-shop) Geoffrey Lupton, another highly influential figure in the Arts and Crafts movement. Thomas lived here between 1908 and 1913. Despite the house and garden offering stunning views across the Weald to the south, Thomas found it difficult to live here because of its extreme exposure to the elements.

The Red House

It's great fun to do some detective work and to find where a figure such as Thomas lived and worked. We can't quite see his writing hut, known as the Bee House, which still stands in the garden next door – but we've been given kind permission to step off the path and into the back garden of 'The Red House' by its present owners.

It's an impressive red brick and tile house, perched right on the lip of the escarpment. The views today are awe-inspiring – 'Sixty miles of South Downs at one glance', as Thomas wrote in his poem 'Wind and Mist' – but the wind got to him in winter, and the mist, and the extraordinary elevation. He felt he was living far too high, up in the clouds, increasingly dis-connected from the ground below. At least it helped him to this powerful realization: 'I did not know it was the earth I loved/ Until I tried to live there in the clouds.'

This line really speaks to me. We can live so much of the time with our head in the clouds. Materially, we try to climb higher in life. Spiritually, we so often go in search of lofty or other-worldly enlightenment. Yet it's that connection with the earth that seems to make Thomas so human. It reminds me, as I stand up here with vertigo looking down upon circling buzzards, to maintain a feel for the ground; a connection with the earth, its flowers and fruits, its seasons and rhythms. Christians worship the God who, in very nature, was down-to-Earth, who walked the way of love – and, as Easter edges into view, we remember also the way of the Cross.

We walk on down the narrow lane that runs along the top of the escarpment, conscious of our steps now, of being earthed. In fact, we spend a few moments synchronizing our breathing with our steps – three steps for the in-breath, three or four for the out-breath – planting our feet on the ground as we go. That phrase 'follow in the footsteps' feels apt, when you're walking. So often, the most spiritually inspiring people – such as Gandhi and Mother Teresa, perhaps – were those willing to get their hands and feet dirty in the process of walking this path of life and faith.

The next junction, a seemingly timeless crossroads with Old Litten Lane, is where Thomas often would have turned left to walk across the hills for a pint at the isolated inn called the White Horse. For us, that treat comes later, but for now we turn right, on to the summit of Shoulder of Mutton Hill and its magnificent vistas.

Shoulder of Mutton Hill

Here, we share the delight of William Cobbett who wrote in his famous book Rural Rides *(1830) about the rigours of travelling this part of southern England on horseback. Cobbett reflects on his arrival at the exact place where we are now standing, about 200 years before us:*

Out we came, all in a moment, at the very edge of the hanger! And, never in all my life, was I so surprised and so delighted! I pulled up my horse, and sat and looked and it was like looking from the top of a castle down into the sea, except that the valley was land and not water …

He adds: 'Those who had so strenuously dwelt on the dirt and dangers of this route had said not a word about the beauties, the matchless beauties of the scenery.'

This breath-taking view across the Weald, to the ridge of the South Downs in the far distance, has probably changed very little over two centuries, apart from the slow but continuous removal of woodland to create land for agriculture and building development.

A short but steep descent from the 'edge of the hanger' brings us to a standing stone that serves as a lasting memorial to Edward Thomas. Following the example of Cobbett, we 'sit and look': at the stone and the distant view, but notice too that we are surrounded by a host of tiny flowers that add a springtime array of colours to the grassy hillside: among them the yellow of cowslips, purple of wood violets, white of wild strawberries and blue of milkwort.

We are intentionally mindful of what we can feel, too: the gentle breeze on our face; the warmth of the turf beneath us; the texture of the grass; the ache in our legs.

The road less taken

The memorial quotes a line from one of Thomas's essays: 'And I rose up, and knew that I was tired, and continued my journey.'

Along that continued journey, the man who was prone to deep melancholy found solace not just in nature but in friendship, too – with the young Robert Frost, who was visiting England from America, hoping to make his name as a poet.

Thomas, who was among the most influential literary critics of his age, became the first to acknowledge the power of Frost's verse, and was instrumental in his transition into a poet of world renown. But Frost returned the favour.

As they cultivated their friendship, covering mile after mile walking and bird-watching, Frost saw in Thomas's prose a poetry that was waiting to be unearthed, and he encouraged him to write lines of verse instead of paragraphs.

The dam burst; Thomas finished 85 poems in the seven months before he enlisted for the war in July 1915, and over 40 from late 1915 to August 1916. He composed many in his head as he walked daily from his final residence below in the village of Steep, up the hill to the Bee House (which he continued to use, after moving).

Perhaps there is something good to be called out of each of us, by a friend.

Perhaps, too, our own eyes can open to the potential of others: to see the poetry within the prose, and to release them to become more fully who they are.

As we make our faltering descent down the hill, we consider quietly the people in our own lives who have seen our potential, and we give thanks for them.

A glimpse of prehistoric times

*On the return leg of our route, Brian suggests that we should try 'a walk of awareness', slowly and silently, to notice more of what's around us. Passing through the woodland of Ashford Chace on a bank that is about head high, one of our group spots something new to many of us: lots of white plant-like structures about 20 centimetres high emerging from the bare soil and covered at the top with many small protuberances. These turn out to be the fertile shoots of a plant called the 'great horsetail' (*Equisetum telmateia*).*

The horsetails, like the ferns, are flowerless and seedless plants that reproduce by spores and also spread via branching underground rhizomes. There are nine British species of Equisetum, *none taller than one and a half metres and with a distinctive appearance of feathery side branches on yellowish stems.*

Horsetails could be described as 'living fossils': much-reduced remnants of a large family of plants that flourished in the era of the dinosaurs. Many of the extinct species were large trees forming extensive Palaeozoic forests and decaying to eventually form the rocks of the Coal Measures. Here, then, before our eyes, is a living reminder of our place within deep time, not just stratified in cliffs such as Kimmeridge, or in charts on a wall, but layered and textured into the countryside around us and renewed every springtime; fresh shoots from such ancient roots.

Another thing we notice is a short section of barbed-wire fence that had originally been stretched against the trunk of a sycamore tree. The growth of the tree over several years has allowed the 'pain' of the barbed wire to be literally absorbed into the trunk of the tree with no obvious signs of ongoing hurt or damage. It speaks to us gently of the healing and restoration that seems to come, most naturally, to nature.

To lose yourself

Walking was therapeutic to Thomas, and is surely helpful – psychologically, emotionally, spiritually – for so many of us. There's that sense of being able to positively lose yourself as you go, and thus, mysteriously, to find yourself in the process. To find yourself calmer, less stressed, more settled. We can feel it, as we begin to loop back to our starting point.

Thomas's poem 'Lights Out' hints at the almost mystical sense of personal surrender we can experience when walking.

> The tall forest towers:
> Its cloudy foliage lowers,
> Ahead, shelf above shelf;
> Its silence I hear and obey
> That I may lose my way
> and myself.

The pace slows, the pulse dawdles, the mind settles. There is, indeed, a silence – to hear and obey. To *obey*. What a word. Only from a poet.

Glimpses of the 'Season of White'

The verges alongside the lanes back to Northfield Wood are full of cow parsley, still green but with flowers waiting to emerge. In the hedges, the fading blackthorn flowers will soon be replaced by a profusion of white hawthorn blossom and the showy flower clusters of wayfaring-trees. With a few warmer days and certainly by the middle of May, we will be celebrating the glorious 'Season of White' in the countryside.

We retrieve our cars from outside the church, for our final port of call lies a few miles north of Steep in the surrounding hills. We're heading to the White Horse, the remote inn also known locally as 'The Pub With No Name' – which makes sense as we spot the metal frame of the empty roadside pub-sign. Thomas was a regular here and he would walk the several miles for his refreshment.

Seeking sanctuary

Oh joy, oh joy! This is the inn where the very first lines of Thomas's very first poem, 'Up in the Wind', began to flow. We find the entrance, bend our heads, and descend a couple of steps into what's now known as the Edward Thomas bar – 'that forest parlour,/Low and small among the towering beeches'.

It's like entering a sanctuary. The windows allow just enough of the fading afternoon light to fall softly, again, upon our day. And like the church we began our walk from, this air feels old, the space set apart; I'm sure that, if they could speak, the tobacco-stained walls and the beams that hang low above would tell us where the man once sat and watched and listened and drank and wrote his very first words.

You have to start somewhere, creatively. You have to *make* that start. Let it flow, like the Source.

Quaffing a pint of real ale in unison after a walk together like this feels like communion. A holy, transcendent moment of togetherness; a quenching of a deeper thirst, the kind of soul thirst that you didn't really know you had until something like this helps to slake it. But the wonder, the mystery, is that it's quenched not through some cosmic idea but ... in this case, fermented hops. The simplest of pleasures.

Take, drink. A moment, through its sharing, that is multiplied. An ending, and a beginning, as we head into Easter and, with it, all the promise of spring.

* * *

Words echo back to us from the newly made memories of today, of walking, of companionship, of laughter, of connection, of love. Thomas wrote powerfully of 'the promise of spring', and today we carry it within us.

Glory be to the Father, indeed. And to the Son, and to the Holy Ghost ... As it was in the beginning, is now, and ever shall be, world without end, amen.

It's time for home.

Activities

- Spend some time quietly in an empty church. Soak in the atmosphere. Sink into the stillness.
- Go in search of bluebells.
- Use the words that Thomas exclaimed as your own prayer: 'Glory be to the Father, and to the Son, and to the Holy Ghost ... As it was in the beginning, is now, and ever shall be, world without end, amen.'
- Trace a river upstream to its source.
- Reflect on what you've received from others, and what you manage to pass on. Notice if there's anything you're tempted to keep back for yourself, and whether you can release 'the flow'.
- Consider your own personal possessions. How much disposable stuff do you consume? Which, of your possessions, was built lovingly to last? How could you shop for quality, not quantity, in the future?

- Make something with your hands. Anything! Make it with loving care.
- Track down the haunt of a favourite author or poet or artist. Try to see the locality through their eyes. Get a sense of how they look at the world, and then try to get a sense of how you look at the world, uniquely.
- Take a slow walk of awareness, and synchronize your breathing with your steps to help you to feel more grounded and centred.
- Encourage a friend by helping them to see their own potential. Seek help from someone else to discern your own!
- Why not write your own poem in response to a walk in the wild? Don't worry about how good it is. You might even like to destroy it afterwards, so that you don't get too worried about whether or not it's of 'value'!
- Go for a really long walk to a country pub with a friend or two, and savour the soulful physicality of simple pleasures.

5

May
For a New Beginning

*A saunter in spring around the grounds and
environs of Mottisfont Abbey*

A monumental London Plane tree offers shelter from some
light spring rain, though it could equally be from the strengthening sun which will make an appearance later in the day.
How welcome, the cover of a tree! (And when do we ever stop
to say thank you?)

Today, we're in the grounds of Mottisfont Abbey, in
Hampshire, and its lawns rejoice in many of these venerable specimens. The largest London Plane in England rises
high above the great house (once an Augustinian priory), its
patchwork bark of greens and browns the pattern of army
camouflage. Meanwhile beech, sycamore, oak and hornbeam
are showing off their varying degrees of spring's exuberantly
green shades; a single, blushing, copper beech is the exception.

For several years, Howard and I have led a series of walking retreats from here, which we've called 'the Spring Saunters', and we're gathered with a group of ten or so people for another, today. We love the word 'saunter', which derives from the French phrase *a la sainte terre*, 'to the holy ground'. It reminds us that there's a different way of moving: not rushing breathlessly from A to B, but making humble, purposeful pilgrimage towards the holy heart of what was already here, before us.

* * *

Whenever we visit Mottisfont, we're reminded of the words of the American writer Rebecca Solnit: 'Sense of place is the sixth sense, an internal compass and map made by memory and spatial perception together.'

Our internal compasses are already twitching with memories of the history of this place, and our many visits to it.

Mottisfont is located on a gravel ridge at the junction of the Rivers Test and Dun in south Hampshire. Throughout history, invaders have used river valleys as the way inland from the coast. In Anglo-Saxon times, it was probably the Jutes who came up the Test Valley from the direction of Southampton and the Solent during the fifth and sixth centuries.

Why did they, like the Romans, and the Iron-, Bronze- and Stone-Age peoples before them, decide to settle here? It's all because of a spring, a crystal-clear stream of water that flows in abundance and has never been known to dry up. In fact, the name 'Mottisfont' means 'a meeting place by a spring'.

Solnit's 'sixth sense' tells us that this is a 'thin place': a term made popular by the revival of Celtic Christian spirituality as a way of describing a place where the veil between Heaven and Earth seems 'thinner'; where we can expect to draw closer to God through the natural world, and find our own place within it, once more.

Pay attention

The sap is rising; life itself now seems to be flooding back into the year like a tide. The words of the poet Mary Oliver remind us of the reverential sense of how we can *be*, and how we might respond, on a day like today: 'Now in the spring I kneel,' she writes in her prose collection *Upstream*. 'I put my face into the packets of violets, the dampness, the freshness, the sense of ever-ness …

'Attention,' she concludes, 'is the beginning of devotion.'

* * *

That simple discipline of 'paying attention' lies at the heart of all contemplative spirituality. Everything seems to flow from here. Through attention, we reconnect.

So before we even take a step, we pause to notice where we are; to breathe the air, to watch, to listen, to use our senses. Instead of clutching smartphones and 'consuming' our surroundings, today we want to be creatures again, within creation. And we need only cradle into the smoothly supportive roots of a great tree, as one of our group now does; or stand quietly watching the nearby river flow; or stare upwards into the space between the branches of the great trees – for the 'outside' world of tree, flower and plant, river, cloud and birdsong to somehow become part of our inner world.

It is *in* our nature, as we are in its.

* * *

The sense of smell is particularly evocative. In her book of 'indigenous wisdom, scientific knowledge and the teaching of plants' *Braiding Sweetgrass*, the Native American botanist Robin Wall Kimmerer writes of how sweetgrass plays a key part within her people's Creation narrative; the story goes that it was the first plant to grow on the earth, and consequently it was honoured as sacred.

'Breathe in its scent,' she writes, 'and you start to remember things you didn't know you'd forgotten.' Its fragrance, she says, is a 'sweet memory'. It connects us to something beyond the day-to-day, to a story that's greater than just our own.

I wonder what it is that *we* don't know we've forgotten. And I wonder what takes us there. The smell of cut grass? The smell of a river in flow? The smell of warm turf?

Our group spends a few extra moments 'breathing the scent' and letting the fragrance of this fresh spring day take us, in a sense, all the way back to the beginning again, when – according to the Judeo-Christian Creation story – 'it was good'. We breathe, to let ourselves relax and to reconnect with something we didn't even know we'd forgotten. It's that sixth sense at work, the intuitive wisdom that reminds us, through such wonders as smell, that we're all part of something more.

Look for the overlooked

And so, from this place of prayerful attentiveness, we start to saunter slowly up along a small, shady path beside a clear stream, which is at some points flowing serenely, and at others babbling away down the hill.

One of our number is especially struck by a thought that bubbles up about the simplicity of being, and she draws upon the flow of the stream for inspiration. 'The stream flows, because that's what a stream does,' she says, wide-eyed. 'And God loves, because that's what God does.'

It's enough to stop us in our tracks again for a few moments of wonder.

* * *

As we continue upstream, Howard reminds us to notice what we might miss, as well – and this is such good practice. Look for the overlooked; keep watch for the insignificant, as well as for the magnificent …

The 600 species of UK birds and 100 species of mammal are far outnumbered by well over 20,000 insects. Add to the latter the multitude of other invertebrates and micro-organisms and the less obvious flora and fauna are much more abundant. They can have a beauty unmatched by larger or more flamboyant organisms. And from a practical perspective, smaller organisms are the vital resource at the base of all food webs.

Damp woodlands and shady stream-sides like this one are favoured by non-flowering plants and their associated communities of animals. The relatively moist, cool conditions that are typical of such habitats allow mosses and ferns to flourish.

Mosses provide shelter for communities of small animals. Among them are the tiny tardigrades, also known as water bears or moss piglets. Minute, eight-legged beasts rarely exceeding one millimetre in length, their resilience is legendary. Tardigrades can survive for decades without water, be cooled to minus 273 and heated to 150 degrees centigrade, be crushed at 6,000 atmospheres pressure or be exposed to 1,000 times more radiation than would kill a human!

* * *

Those tardigrades, when magnified, look as if they were dreamed up by George Lucas for a walk-on role in *Star Wars*; all angular, armour-plated body with an unfeasibly cute face. We're reminded of the words of the psalmist: 'Praise him, you small creatures!' (Psalm 148.10–13). And surely these tiny creatures, just through their very presence, provide a uniquely inspiring expression of divine creativity.

The tardigrades may be almost supernaturally resilient, but a recent gut-wrenching United Nations report into the state of global biodiversity suggests that over a million different species are now in danger of extinction. The vast majority of these do not have the same rock-star appeal as the great, noble and threatened beasts such as the tiger and rhinoceros – they are the unnoticed and seemingly unremarkable plants and creatures – yet they are crucial to the whole of life on Earth.

As the ecologist Sandra Díaz told *National Geographic*, 'The tremendous variety of living species ... that make up our "life-supporting safety net" provide our food, clean water, air, energy, and more. Not only is our safety net shrinking, it's becoming more threadbare and holes are appearing.'

Howard is a fan and supporter of the charity Bug Life, which looks after a swathe of these unnoticed species, and he reads us a sobering line from Sir David Attenborough, who is another supporter: 'If we and the rest of the back-boned animals were to disappear overnight, the rest of the world would get on pretty well. But if the invertebrates were to disappear, the world's ecosystems would collapse.'

Unfurling ferns

A little further upstream, as sunlight begins to break through, we're able to enjoy the refreshing sight of a clump of ferns, some of which are tightly coiled, while others are at different stages of unfurling. The brown-green spirals are like fractals, and speak eloquently of the mystery of life.

In fact, the Maori have a word, *koru*, to describe the coil of their own native silver fern, which is not dissimilar to these we're looking at here. The circular outer edge of the coil, for the Maori, represents the perpetual motion of life, while the inner spiral evokes our return to the centre, to the Source of life.

Such symbolism is especially pertinent for this time of year. Each spring, we're another year older; time has passed, and seems to pass by faster as the years accumulate. And yet, we also return every spring to this very same point: to the time-honoured seasonal miracle of new life emerging.

'Unfurl yourself into the grace of beginning,' writes John O'Donohue in his powerful poem 'For a New Beginning'. It's a gorgeous line. The ferns remind us to unfurl physically, emotionally, spiritually. We hold out our arms for a moment, and stretch upwards and outwards. I'm sure we're all standing a little taller as we head off. Not that there's any rush; the ferns will unfurl when it's right, in their own time.

Close to the source

As we reach the top of a gentle slope, and emerge through the dappled shade of a mature hornbeam tree, we find ourselves standing in quiet reverence at the source of the stream: the well-spring, the ancient meeting point. It's the reason that all of this place – the great house, the world-famous vintage rose garden of Mottisfont, even the village itself – is here.

Channelling up through a stone circle eight feet (2.4 m) or so in diameter, the spring's aquamarine water looks utterly still – just like a well. As a fly lands upon it, the glassy surface ripples. In fact, the only clue that 900 litres of water per minute are pouring up and out from this pool is the stream we have followed, which curves out and away down the hill from the well (its shape reminding us, as we watch, of the curve of the uncoiling fern).

A short, sharp waterfall close to this bend accentuates the power of the overflow, and it's not hard to draw direct comparison with the spiritual 'overflow' that we can experience when we return to the Source, as we found in Steep.

We pause, for several minutes, in stillness at this place; not thinking or trying too hard, but observing the flow, and letting it release something of our own inner Source, the living waters that can overflow us, to bring refreshment to the world around us.

* * *

We've invited our participants to respond creatively when they feel the urge, today, by writing a haiku – the Japanese short form of poetry. Fiona reads hers, and it seems to encapsulate something we all sense:

> Still waters run deep
> So they say: but I say, here,
> Deep waters run still.

At Mottisfont, many visitors walk straight past the humble well-spring without realizing it's even there, as they head for the more obvious attractions. And it makes us wonder, if our inner life were like the grounds of this beautiful place, where we would find the well-spring, and how often we would return to it, to draw deeply from its energy, its wisdom, its nourishment, its life.

We are standing on holy ground

As we saunter on towards the brow of a hill and the edge of a field close by, the vista opens up, to reveal a sloping field of shin-high grasses billowing in the breeze. It's as if this dry stretch of nature has its own flow, too; like water, it waves and ripples, an ocean of grasses and flowers, in continuous fluid movement, yet exuding a sense of inner stillness, just like the well-spring.

The sight is framed by the edge of the South Downs which end just beyond, before they sink underground. We've come to walk appreciatively through this meadow, to savour an increasingly rare experience; after all, when was the last time you found yourself within the clover and wild flowers of a meadow in springtime?

* * *

'"Meadow" is surprisingly strict in its meaning and is from the Old English word meaning "to mow". A meadow is a place where grass and flowers are grown for hay, the dry winter fodder for livestock. A meadow is not a natural habitat; it is a relationship between nature, man and beast. At its best, it is also equilibrium, artistry.' So writes John Lewis-Stempel in his delightful book, Meadowland: The Private Life of an English Field.

A slow walk through a meadow on a fine day in May is an uplifting experience of unexpected diversity and delight. But again, it's worth looking for the overlooked, which in this case is the hidden world of wonder in the soil beneath our feet: the most complex, undervalued and vital of all ecosystems.

The World Wildlife Fund describes our soil poetically as 'the fragile skin that anchors life on Earth [and is] among the most precious resources to humans'. Yet our soil is under huge threat. A report from the United Nations Food and Agriculture Organization suggests that about a third of the world's soil has already been degraded. This is caused by chemical-heavy farming, deforestation (which increases erosion), and global heating. It has been estimated that only 60 years of farming are left if soil degradation continues at the current rate.

It's astonishing to think that, in good meadow soil, just one cubic metre is likely to contain as many living organisms as there are people on the Earth. These can range in size from badgers and moles, through a myriad of smaller animals such as worms and invertebrates, to billions of microscopic bacteria and fungi – the champions of nutrient recycling.

Huge numbers of filamentous fungi called mycorrhizae, for example, live in the soil in a mutually beneficial association with plant roots. The fungus greatly extends the capacity of roots to absorb water and minerals. In return, it feeds on sugars made in the leaves and transported down the stem of the plant, leaking out through the roots. This example of symbiosis reminds us that win–win situations are always possible.

* * *

The mystics would remind us that, wherever we go, we are standing on holy ground. If only we could treat it as such! (We are minded that the Sabbath principle of the Bible was not just for the benefit of people, but to bring restoration to the *land* every seventh year by leaving it fallow instead of exhausted.)

As the poet Elizabeth Barrett Browning puts it:

Earth's crammed with heaven
And every common bush afire with God,
But only he who sees takes off his shoes.

And with that in mind, we do indeed take off our shoes to walk through the meadow, savouring each step as we go. This is reconnection, and it seems to matter more than ever (97 per cent of British meadowland has now been lost, according to recent statistics).

It feels indulgent, in a sense, to give ourselves permission to *enjoy* this moment, given those statistics. Yet the reconnection has to start with each of us, individually. Surely we each need, in our own way, to learn to walk with love upon the Earth once more. And unless we learn to love this meadow, these grasses, the insects that we see as we walk slowly, the clover, even the dandelions ... then we'll surely not learn to fight for them, either.

'Every step is a miracle', as the mindfulness expert Thich Nhat Hanh puts it, and he's surely right. 'The real miracle is not to walk on fire or to fly, but to walk upon the Earth.'

Enlightened in a coppice

We continue onwards, mindfully – and passing through a wooden gate, we reluctantly pop our shoes back on, and head out along a quintessential may-lined Hampshire lane, not a car in sight today, before turning right along a rutted track which leads us into woodland.

Sunlight filters on to the floor of a clearing, where we pause to experience the sheer volume of birdsong – a truly hypnotic, uplifting cacophony. No wonder doctors are beginning to 'prescribe' nature! In fact, a recent major study (reported in the *Guardian* newspaper) has concluded that it takes just two cumulative hours a week of being within nature, whether in the park, or in the woods, or at the beach, to make a significantly positive impact on humans emotionally, physically and psychologically. It's predicted that, before long, two hours in nature will join the five-a-day of fruit-and-veg and the 150 minutes of exercise a week as official health advice. Liz, who works at a children's hospice, shares with me that within this natural context she feels able 'to listen to the ancient wisdom of nature, and to be reminded that my life is sustained by this beautiful Earth'.

We're not just here to listen to the birdsong, however. We're also here to see how the National Trust has reintroduced the ancient art of coppicing, and to learn more about the mutual flourishing of nature and humanity.

* * *

Coppicing is a sustainable form of woodland management that was widespread until the mid-1800s. It involves the repetitive felling of deciduous trees to just above ground level, in order to stimulate new growth. The trees respond to felling by sending up multiple stems from the cut stump. The new stems usually grow fast and straight which allows them to have a variety of uses, from the production of charcoal for smelting and the extraction of liquors for tanning to the supply of various types of wood for building and faggots for domestic fires. Nothing was wasted from wood harvested by coppicing.

Most of our native trees can be coppiced but the commonly used species are hazel, sweet chestnut, ash and oak. The advantage of hazel is that it's harvested after only eight years (rather than twenty for other species).

The National Trust has reintroduced hazel coppicing into woods at Mottisfont and, in order to allow mature trees to be harvested annually, the woods are divided into eight compartments, with one cut each winter. The larger-cut sections of timber are burnt to produce charcoal and the finest twigs bundled up to strengthen river banks.

As coppicing declined over the last hundred years, ancient woodlands were either grubbed up and replaced with conifer plantations, removed to create building sites and additional farmland, or left to become overgrown. This was disastrous for the wildlife that had, over previous centuries, adapted to the types of habitat that coppiced woodland creates.

Crucially, coppicing allows more light to reach the woodland floor, which in turn means that traditional flowering plants of ancient woodlands can return: native bluebell, wood violet,

*primrose, wood anemone and many others. With a wider vari-
ety of plant life comes the return of invertebrates and all the
other animals up the woodland food web that depend on plants.*

*An iconic butterfly that has returned to Mottisfont's coppiced
woods is the silver-washed fritillary. Its caterpillars feed on
wood violet in the lighter, younger compartments.*

*Coppicing a wood greatly enhances biodiversity and it's
encouraging to note that in recent years there has been a modest revival of the practice.*

* * *

John Lewis-Stempel mentioned the 'artistry' of maintaining
meadows, and coppicing is clearly an art form, too. Without
the help of people, the woodland would not flourish in quite
the same way. Humans *can* be a positive force for good, if
we find our flow within the rhythms of creation, and perhaps
we should reflect more intentionally on the way we can bring
about mutual flourishing – a form of communion – wherever
we put our hands to work.

In fact, the practice has much to teach us personally. Looking down at the woodland floor, we contemplate the seeds that
have lain dormant for decades, and reflect on how they can be
activated by the light that floods in after undergrowth has been
cleared. Some areas of our life have become so overgrown that
it's hard for any light to find its way through. But who knows
what seeds are lying dormant, waiting to be germinated, if we
make space in our life to let the light back in?

In that copse, with the sun falling on our faces, it feels a little
easier, a little more natural, to yield to the process of letting
go, of clearing space in our schedules, of making room for the
unexpected.

* * *

And to think that nothing in the process is wasted – not even
a branch! We find ourselves standing before stacks of hazel

wood all lined up, of different thicknesses, each to be used in different ways. It's a powerfully moving moment. Could it be that – just as in nature's economy – nothing is wasted in God's economy, either? That everything is used to bring about good in the end, even (and often especially) from out of the pain of loss?

Standing in stillness, amid the harmonious song of blackcaps and robins and blackbirds, we reach out to touch the warm, smooth bark of the hazel. This is an unspeakably moving place to find ourselves, and the moment sort of catches up with us. I don't know how a pile of wood can do this; all I know is: it does. Tears are gently released.

And as we quietly leave the wood for our final port of call, it's fair to say a number of us feel different; shifted, somehow. I can't find the words myself, but Wendy, a counsellor, shares that she has encountered 'something I've never experienced in that way before, a moment of total connection to the universe'.

Along the river

Leaving the woods, we're heading half a mile or so back down the lane to pay homage to an ancient oak; but just before we get there, we take a moment to pause on a bridge over a widening stretch of a tributary to the River Test. This is pristine English nature at its finest; and, in the presence of such clear water, gratitude flows, and smiles break out in all directions. What on earth is as heavenly as water such as this?

The chalk streams of southern England are a precious national asset, as they comprise the majority found anywhere on the planet. Rivers such as the Test create a rare and beautiful local landscape, characterized in the middle and upper reaches by crystal clear, fast flowing and well-oxygenated water. They are home, like the soil, to vast numbers of plants and animals that live beneath the surface in a complex aquatic ecosystem.

At the top of the food web are fish, famously trout and salmon, but also many other species: grayling, pike, eels, bullheads and stickleback, to name but a few. Millions of invertebrates provide food for the fish, and live in the submerged plants of the river and in the gravel and silt of the bed itself. This is a miniature, hidden but vital part of the natural world.

Fly fishing for trout and salmon on the Hampshire chalk streams begins officially on 3 April but, for the majority of keen anglers, the season starts on 1 May. The tradition of the later date has become established over the years because the month of May sees the first big hatches of a main food source of the fish: the appropriately named mayfly. Simon Cooper, in his fascinating book Life of a Chalkstream, *writes:*

> *Whichever way you cut it, the mayfly is the iconic chalkstream insect. It defines the most exciting moments in the fishing calendar. It is proof that the chalkstreams are the most perfect rivers ever created. It is the moment when sometimes you have to step back, shut out the rest of the world and watch in awe to simply accept that nature is utterly and completely amazing.*

It is indeed! Typically, mayfly and related chalkstream species such as caddis fly and stone fly spend two years as nymphs in the weed and the river bed, then hatch to live just 24 hours as adults, mating and laying their eggs back in the river. The nymphs of caddis fly protect themselves with exquisitely crafted protective cases made of tiny stones or minute pieces of wood and reed which they somehow manage to weave around their bodies.

Continuing our saunter, just over the bridge and a short way down a green lane, we reach the oldest living organism in Hampshire: the Mottisfont Oak.

The wild divinity of an ancient oak

The Mottisfont Oak is 1,000 years old, plus or minus 200 years, and grows in a small meadow alongside the tributary.

Scanning this part of the valley landscape, you would probably miss its true grandeur among the other mature trees. It is squat, with a good number of leafy branches in summer, but it is not until you get close enough to see the massive bole of the tree that its great age becomes clear.

The girth of approximately 37 feet (11.5 m) is impressive when set alongside the categorization of the girth of oak trees described in Natural England's 'Veteran Trees' guide: a ten foot (3 m) girth makes a tree 'potentially interesting'; a fifteen-foot (4.5 m) girth 'valuable for conservation' and a twenty-foot (6 m) girth 'truly ancient'. Perhaps we need another superlative for the Mottisfont Oak: 'magnificently millennial'!

* * *

If you pause beside an ancient tree for long enough, it may well yield all sorts of secrets. Right here, we struggle to take in the fact that it's *this* old! Its trunk is gnarled like an over-sized elephant's leg. Many of its branches are scarred; some are broken off, bare or storm damaged.

And yet, here in May, is the wonder: that it is covered with new, fresh leaves, as new as life itself. Don't let anyone tell you that you cannot be a continual site for new life. The experience and wisdom of older age do not have to preclude fresh seasons of growth; this is not a zero-sum game.

So we stand close to the tree, in a quiet reverie. Here, the ego is quickly quietened. You cannot hope to impress a tree like this, so why even try? This oak simultaneously dives down towards the Source through its roots, and rises upwards, through its branches, to the skies. John O'Donohue refers to the 'wild divinity' of trees, and I'd like to think, standing before this specimen, that it calls to something of the wild divinity in me, in us. You are a wild soul, despite it all. We were made for more than simply building widgets.

Robin Wall Kimmerer says that, in the science of botany, we're taught to ask, 'What is that?' about a tree or a plant. Meanwhile, the indigenous wisdom of her Native American upbringing teaches her to ask of a tree or a plant the far more personal question, 'Who are you?' Perhaps, in learning to ask this of a tree, we can learn to ask it better of ourselves, as well.

The oak – *she* – is also a magnificent lesson in surface area – of leaf and branch and root combining to ensure that as much of the sun's energy, and the earth's goodness, is absorbed as possible.

Would that we could become as absorbent. We stand as still as the tree, to sense our own surface area, and to absorb more of the goodness of this day, and more of the goodness of its Creator's love, which feels, in this moment, as warm as sunshine.

* * *

The tree is a haven for wildlife and hosts a large community of other organisms, not least colonies of bats and many birds, including barn owls and kestrels. But again it is the less obvious fauna and flora that are so special. The Woodland Trust, in a 2006 report on ancient trees and biodiversity, notes: 'The special features of ancient trees which make them unique as wildlife habitat are the exceptionally species-rich communities associated with wood decay, the bare surfaces of the trunk and boughs and the roots.'

There are literally thousands of species that depend on these features and, because of the general scarcity of ancient trees in the countryside, a very high proportion feature on lists of our rarest and most threatened species. The types of species are predominantly small and rather obscure: fungi, beetles, flies, lichens and mosses.

It's wonderful to think what a tree such as the Mottisfont Oak has heard, seen and experienced over its 1,000 or more years. Conversations among the monks from the Priory, as they walked along the river bank, surely; the comings and goings of the many plants and animals that have called it home; courting couples using its hollow trunk for secret rendezvous; violent storms that shattered some of its branches, and the tranquil peace of an afternoon in spring. This is the natural world at its most awesome, but in an understatedly English way.

* * *

Just opposite, on the other side of the track along which we've wandered, the clear waters of the River Test are in flow, throwing shafts of reflected sunlight back up into a gently weeping willow. Overhead there is a cloud burst of swallows, martins and swifts. Blue above, green below, and the birds engaging in another mesmerising example of flow; circling, looping, twisting, swooping, diving ...

As we make to leave, we notice two small things. First, the sound of chicks from within the canopy of the oak. Such a moving juxtaposition: the ancient form of life sheltering the most recently hatched.

And then we spot an oak sapling that has been planted close by. It is protected from nibbling deer by some plastic tubing. She may – who knows? – be standing here many centuries from now, long after we are gone and forgotten, rising tall, roots sinking deeper, poised and in touch with the light of life and the darkness of the soil below ...

And sheltering the faintest memory of a group of saunterers, perhaps, who walked this way in quiet pilgrimage, back in the beginning, when she was very, very young.

Activities

- Pay attention. For 'attention is the beginning of devotion', as Mary Oliver says.
- Stand quietly in a green space, relax, breathe more slowly and deeply, and enjoy being 'here'. 'Breathe the scent', as Robin Wall Kimmerer suggests. Let it transport you.
- Look out for the small and less significant things that you might otherwise miss; look up and down as well as straight ahead. Fix your attention upon something you notice for an extended time, simply observing it without agenda or preconception.
- Unfurl yourself physically, like a fern.

- Write a haiku. The typical form of the short poem is three lines long, using five syllables for the first line, seven syllables for the second, and then five syllables for the last line. Use this as a way of distilling the essence of something you've heard, seen or connected with.
- Find a meadow. Look closely at the plants and the soil around you, and try a short walk with bare feet. What do you reconnect with? (NB: Check for ticks afterwards! They are on the rise, and carry the risk of Lyme Disease.)
- Try to find some actively coppiced woodland that is accessible, and meditate upon some of the themes we touch on above.
- Locate an ancient tree, and spend some time with it.
- For lightweight, laminated, beautifully illustrated and relatively inexpensive identification guides to all the main flora, fauna and habitats of Britain, you may like to look at the Field Studies Council Guides, available from many bookshops and from www.field-studies-council.org.

6

June
Let There Be Light!

*Pepperbox Hill, and a walk through Salisbury,
on the summer solstice*

The longest day. Revered, from way, way back in the beginning, when God saw the light, and it was good.

The alarm was set, but I didn't need it. It's funny how the body wakes you if you ask it to. A flask of tea, a light jacket, a notebook, and I'm slipping out and up the road. There's a magical stillness out here which evokes earliest memories of rising before dawn to drive to the West Country for our annual family holiday; the fierce excitement of childhood blazing like a light within.

In the east, a brightness. And just up the road, an unexpected sight: a man, mid-forties, in shorts and a crumpled T-shirt, eyes bleary, hair all over the place, standing by the side of the road, looking east across a field. Waiting. Watching. Like every other man, woman and child who has risen to watch the sun on the solstice. Here is humanity itself, it feels, orienting itself towards the light, almost by instinct. The field he's staring through is about to be developed as a housing estate; heavy equipment lies sleeping amid the weeds and grasses. I nod to humanity as I get closer. 'We won't be able to see this view next year,' he offers, with regret.

I follow the path that leads to my local nature reserve, Barton Meadows; two fields that are set aside within the encroaching development. These are ring-fenced and being restored to meadow, and poppies are peeping up through the remnants of the farmer's final crop, blood-red petals, crumpled inwards like crepe paper, waiting, too, for their own touch of light, for their own re-awakening.

A distant, waking thrum of trains, planes, cars – even at this time – as the human world revs into what we think is life; but above it all, with hopeful resistance, a rising volume of skylarks, one of only a handful of birds that sing while they're flying. Imagine singing like that as you ran or walked. Sometimes, I wish I had the nerve to express myself more fully, more skylark-fully.

Softly purple thistles stretch, and feathery barley seems to flow in waves towards me like a green and gentle sea. Seagulls plough an aerial furrow above the fields, tracing ancient pathways, invisible to the human eye, purposefully through the sky.

This day is as old as a universe and as young as a newborn. And here is a five-bar gate, and a five-bar gate always seems to offer an invitation. 'Stop. Lean. Watch.' A perfect point at which to glimpse this first sight of the sun, pouring over the distant downs for a few pulsating moments like liquid gold.

While it's low on the horizon you can better feel the speed of its movement – or ours, around it. We're part of a creation that is flowing and ebbing, falling and rising, spinning and turning and joyfully expanding, and I am here to see it, and I am here within it, and I am here as part of it.

Let there be light.

Pepperbox Hill

After Brian's early rise, our plan is to meet to walk at Pepper-box Hill near Salisbury, before heading into the city itself to find an urban green space. We turn off the A36 Southampton to Salisbury road, driving up a steep hill shaded by beech trees to a small car park on Pepperbox Hill, now cared for by the National Trust.

A chalk track can be seen clearly leading east towards Dean Hill, which is an ancient pathway known as the South Hampshire Way. You are unlikely to find it on modern maps because parts of the route have disappeared under farmland and, sadly, it is not a long-distance footpath. However, the route can be traced from Winchester in a west-south-westerly direction to the Iron Age fort at Merdon Castle near Hursley, then via Braishfield and a crossing of the River Test at Kimbridge to the south side of the Dun Valley. Here the South Hampshire Way passes another Iron Age settlement at Lockerley and then becomes a footpath along the ridge of Dean Hill to the amazing vistas here at Pepperbox Hill, and beyond.

As with most questions about prehistory, there is no final answer as to why this ancient path was established. But, intriguingly, it is possible that it dates far back to Stone Age times over 10,000 years ago. The South Hampshire Way, it is thought, was used to transport Portland chert to a stone tool factory at Dunbridge, close to the junction of the Dun and Test river valleys near Mottisfont. Many well-preserved axes, arrow heads and other Stone Age tools made of Portland chert have been discovered in gravel workings at Dunbridge.

There is also a theory that, even before the Stone Age, the very oldest trackways through the 'wildwood' of England (defined by the natural historian Oliver Rackham as 'wholly natural wood-land unaffected by Neolithic or later civilization) were created by herds of wild cattle finding their way to new pastures.

The place has a pervasive feeling of mystery and some stupendous views. Five miles to the north we can see the ele-gant spire of Salisbury Cathedral rising above the woods of the Wiltshire Downs.

The compass

Another five-bar gate. Corn, hay fields, hedgerows, undulations in the chalk downs like the surface movements of a still but slopping sea.

Howard pulls out a gorgeous old compass to check our bearings. It was passed on by his dad, he explains, who was given it in turn from *his* dad, Walter. Walter was a carpenter sent to France during the First World War to help with building the wooden support structures that held up the trenches.

Wow. I wonder what we pass on, and pass down? Immediately I'm thinking about my own most treasured object, a little carving of a Spitfire, whittled from an old penny-piece by a German prisoner-of-war who was set to work in Kentish hop-fields where he met my grandfather. Grandpa entrusted me with it when I was a boy. Perhaps the entrustment was a greater gift than the Spitfire.

The pointer on the compass trembles, as if in excitement, and as we get our bearings I realize how rarely I know which direction I'm facing. The swallows and swifts, wheeling high above like Spitfires in a dog-fight, have that enviable, almost incredible instinct to know where home is.

We may not have the luxury of an inbuilt homing device, like migratory birds; but we do, wonderfully, have the instinct of the soul, which reminds us of a different kind of 'home', if we let it. And resting awhile by this gate, before wandering slowly to find a nearby spot to share a simple picnic breakfast, my soul stirs again. The place, the company, the sense of peace ...

'Look at all those tiny flowers,' Howard beams, pointing to the most delicate carpet of colours which are best viewed from down here where we've now settled, in the grass; a vista I had hardly registered within my 'bigger picture' field of vision. Behold, another world.

Summer abundance and the naming of plants

You have to get down on your hands and knees to really appreciate the abundance and the beauty of the tiny flowering plants that grow on chalk grassland and the organisms that live on them. We record over 20 different species of plants in a very short time. These are vital food plants for caterpillars and a wide range of other insects including grasshoppers, bugs, beetles and ants that thrive in these habitats.

Many flowering plants found on these chalk grasslands have intriguing names; among them lady's bedstraw and self-heal. Before plants and animals were given their characteristic two Latin names (one for the genus and another for the species), they were known by their common, local names. The more names a plant had around the country, the greater the number of uses it is likely to have had in medicine, cooking and other aspects of everyday life.

Galium verum – lady's bedstraw – is a good example, with at least 20 different common names. It is a straggling plant found in dry, open grassy places which looks like golden candyfloss when in flower. Smelling of honey and then of hay when dried out, lady's bedstraw was typically mixed with bracken, covered with a sheet and used like a mattress for sleeping. Once this bedding got too verminous it could easily be burnt and replaced. Extracts from the plant were also used as a styptic to stop bleeding and, like rennet, to coagulate milk. A warm footbath with an extract from the flowers could ease the sore feet of tired travellers and, in the Highlands of Scotland, a red dye was obtained from its roots.

Self-heal, or Prunella vulgaris, also had about 20 common names including blue curls, heart o' the earth, pickpocket, prince's feather and touch-and-heal. It was used to ease sore throats and to heal wounds. Before the arrival of synthetic drugs and modern pharmacies, it was to the woods, the hedges, the hillsides and, in cities, the physic garden that people would have come to gather plants and obtain the extracts to be used for the treatment of illness and a host of other purposes.

One of the commonest prostrate flowering plants on Pepper-

box Hill is bird's-foot trefoil. Its little clusters of yellow flowers are dotted in large numbers across the chalkland sward. The name is derived from the small black seed pods that end in a claw, a feature that can be recognized in several of more than 70 common names: cat's claw, dead-man's fingers, old woman's toe-nails and crowfeet ...

* * *

If there is a less conspicuous wealth of flora and fauna beneath our feet, we can certainly see summer's abundance of vegetation in the surrounding hedgerows and woodland. Everything seems to be happening at this time of year, with flowers still blooming in profusion, even as seeds and fruits are beginning to form. Wild thyme creates purple mounds over the ant-hills, wild roses shower the hedges with their simple but elegant pink flowers and privet splashes the borders of the South Hampshire Way with brilliant white.

The still June air is thick with the slightly doubtful smell of privet, described by Richard Mabey in Flora Britannica *as 'a sweetish smell overlaid with the fishy odour familiar in hawthorn blossom'. Small green fruits are already forming on the hawthorn and blackberry bushes, dense clusters of seeds hang on the ash trees, while wild clematis attempts to overwhelm everything in its path.*

We sense a season of plenty.

Parker J. Palmer, in his book Let Your Life Speak, *contrasts summer's typical keynote of abundance in the natural world with human nature, which seems to regard perpetual scarcity as the law of life. He writes:*

If I hoard possessions, it is because I believe that there are not enough to go round. If I struggle with others over power, it is because I believe that power is limited. If I become jealous in relationships, it is because I believe that when you get too much love, I will be short-changed.

The key to living an abundant life, he argues, is to come together in community with others to celebrate and share our common store. Whether the apparently scarce resource is money or power or love, the true law of life is that we generate more of whatever seems scarce by trusting its supply and passing it around.

'Summer is the season when all the promisory notes of autumn and winter and spring come due, and each year the debts are repaid with compound interest,' he says. Sitting on Pepperbox Hill here in high summer, we let these words sink into our consciousness and commit to living more effectively according to the wisdom of sharing life's abundance.

Let there be light

Perhaps most abundant of all, on this extraordinary June day, is the light. Hardly a cloud is to be seen, and, sitting here on the downs, drenched in sunlight, it strikes me, as we chat about the spiritual relationship between 'light' and 'life', that we've a lot to thank William Tyndale for.

Tyndale inspires me: he's the courageous, creative man who was the first to translate the Bible from the original Hebrew and Greek into English, while on the run as an enemy of both the English state and the Pope. There's a statue of him in Whitehall Gardens, London, which I visited with a retreat group recently.

Some very familiar phrases in our English language are down to him, as they flowed from his pen through translation into wider common usage. We've Tyndale to thank for 'under the sun', 'signs of the times', 'my brother's keeper', 'fall flat on his face', 'the land of the living', 'pour out one's heart', 'the apple of his eye', 'go the extra mile', 'the parting of the ways', and so many more.

But the phrase of his that resonates for me so powerfully on this, the longest day: 'Let there be light!' So together, Howard and I sit and read the very opening lines of Tyndale's Bible, words that were crafted 500 years ago, which reach back to the very first moments of the very first morning, and thence reach all the way forward, to us, here, now, on the side of this hill. We read them slowly, and with renewed wonder:

> In the begynnynge God created heaven and erth. The erth was voyde and emptie ad darcknesse was vpon the depe and the spirite of god moved vpon the water. Than God sayd: let there be lyghte and there was lyghte. And God sawe the lyghte that it was good: and devyded the lyghte from the darcknesse and called the lyghte daye and the darcknesse nyghte: and so of the evenynge and mornynge was made the fyrst daye.

Down into Salisbury

We have chosen to drive on a short way to Salisbury as part of our June saunter. It's an opportunity to visit an urban green space, and will bring us alongside another of Hampshire's matchless chalk streams, the River Avon, which flows through the city.

We park up in Salisbury and walk towards the city centre alongside the River Avon, the route taking us through The Maltings, where Sergei and Yulia Skripal were first spotted by passers-by after they'd been poisoned. Times of darkness can visit communities and individuals unexpectedly. We're mindful of how we can each bring a sense of light within darkness, if we choose, and, on this solstice day, we pause to pray for the city and its communities, before moving on.

Heading to the precincts of the cathedral through an ancient city gate, the scene that greets us is breath-taking: the tower and steeple rising over 400 feet (123 m), the tallest in England, and 'darting up into the sky like a needle', as the painter John Constable once put it.

The scene below, however, is not quite as uplifting, with the usually verdant green lawns of the Cathedral Close conspicuously parched brown after the driest June for over 40 years.

Sheltering love

As we find respite from the now blistering sun under a small apple tree, our thoughts turn, quite naturally, to the climate emergency, and species extinction. The dial is being turned up on the thermostat of Planet Earth – in Saddleworth, fires are scorching the northern moors, while wildfires seem to be rampaging across the world, from Australia to the USA to Greece.

What can we do, we wonder, when it seems as if the climate is blazing out of control? Mercifully, movements such as Extinction Rebellion, involving ordinary, everyday people, have begun to show that there *are* courageous, creative and non-violent ways to disrupt busyness-as-usual and to bring the climate emergency into the full solar glare of public awareness.

The quietly powerful presence of the Swedish teenager Greta Thurnberg, too – who began with a personal strike from school, and who now finds herself a global figurehead on the front cover of *Time* magazine – has brought inspiration to a generation of young and old alike, including the 83-year-old grandfather Phil Kingston, who climbed on to the roof of a Docklands Light Railway train in London, with four other members of Christian Climate Action, to disrupt access to London's financial district, Canary Wharf.

He sat up there eating his sandwiches, before being arrested. 'I don't like having to break the law,' he told the media. 'I don't do this lightly. But what other option do we have?' He spoke about his faith in relation to his action, too: 'Being a Christian is about sharing the love of God with others. Although the people at Canary Wharf may not appreciate it, this was an act of love for my children and grandchildren, and for the children and grandchildren of the people working at Canary Wharf.'

You're never too young, it seems, to make a difference, or too old.

* * *

While it's incontrovertible that we need a mass movement towards profound personal and corporate lifestyle change, there's something else, too, that is foundational, and achievable, according to the nature writer Michael McCarthy, author of a simultaneously apocalyptic and hopeful book on climate change called *The Moth Snowstorm*.

He argues that one of our greatest weapons in defence of nature, ultimately, is *joy*. That's because joy, and its close cousin wonder, lead us to a deepening love for nature. And the word love is crucial. It's not a consumerist love 'of' nature, in the way we might love chocolate. It's a love *for*. If we do not stop to delight in nature, then we will never learn to love it; and when we do not love it, we'll not just lose it, but we'll play our part actively, albeit often ignorantly, in destroying it.

Put positively, taking the time to get outside is not an indulgence. Attention is the beginning of devotion, remember. You are fighting back; nurturing a love for creation is a prerequisite of the battle we all now face.

Delightfully, the sound of children playing behind us breaks our concentration, laughter erupting, and we turn to see kids in bare feet blowing bubbles, tearing around without a care and savouring this precious open space at the heart of the city. And their joy is enough to provoke joy in us both.

Carving space

Standing beneath the great west front of the cathedral, we gaze up in awe at the amazing stone carving that has adorned this outside wall since the fourteenth century. There are six tiers of statues with a total of 79 figures representing Christ, the Apostles, Old Testament patriarchs and prophets, angels and archangels.

The meticulous craft work is a lasting tribute to the skills of the stone masons who have worked at the cathedral for over 700 years. Each figure is a work of art, a miracle that has emerged from solid rock and a fulfilment of the words

*attributed to Michelangelo: 'Every block of stone has a statue
inside it and it is the task of the sculptor to discover it.'*

Sacred space, inside and out

*Our cathedrals are inspiring places of shelter and sanctuary, not
just for the human community but also for peregrine falcons.
These magnificent birds provide an excellent opportunity to
spot a fearsomely wild creature from within the urban environment, as the cliff dwellers have adapted to using tall buildings
for nesting in our towns and cities.*

*There were nesting pairs here at Salisbury Cathedral between
1864 and 1953, but there followed a long absence due to per-
secution and the use of pesticides which drove them away from
the south. For several decades, peregrines were endangered and
retreated to the north and west of the UK. Happily, they have
been spreading back, returning to Salisbury in 2014, where
mating pairs successfully raised and fledged chicks. Peregrines
have been here ever since.*

*This amazing bird of prey is among the fastest of predators
on Earth. Its teardrop-shaped body is supremely aerodynamic,
perfect for diving at speeds of 200 miles per hour to catch its
prey in flight. The force of air would explode its lungs were it
not for the 'baffles' in its nostrils – small cones that protrude
to deflect shockwaves of air away from the nasal passage; the
design is now 'bio-mimicked' in jet engines. It's an exhilarating
sight to watch a peregrine in flight; and if you can't spot one,
the cathedral webcam has a live feed of its nesting site.*

* * *

It's tempting to think that our cathedrals are a little more
'sacred' because they have been sites of Christian worship and
ministry for so many centuries, and are so magnificent. Certainly, the building here in Salisbury is awe-inspiring. But the
poet Wendell Berry challenges our cultural idea that church
represents the 'sacred' space in our culture, while all else is

'secular'. There is no such thing as an 'unsacred' place, as he suggests in his poem 'How to Be a Poet': 'only sacred places and desecrated places'.

We think of all the natural places that have touched us deeply and connected us to God, all of which are undoubtedly 'sacred' in their own way, including the many cathedral-esque trees that have towered over us, on our walks so far together. 'The earth is the Lord's,' writes the psalmist. And, we might add, the Earth is my place of worship.

Here in the largest cathedral cloisters in the country, the twelfth-century arcades form an appropriately soul-stirring inside/outside space, with covered arches opening invitingly on to a central outdoor lawn (complete with mighty cedar tree). The light floods in, but a stone-cooled breeze today provides balm. This space seems to exemplify perfectly the flow of 'the sacred' between the Earth and the Church!

So it's here we choose to spend an extended time in personal stillness, and we practise doing nothing but watching the light fall upon the stone pillars.

* * *

Even though there's a cacophony of visiting school pupils, we begin to settle into the space as if it's home.

Light and shade sit with each other, a holy union of ancient and perpetual difference, the one defining and celebrating the other. It has been ever thus, since God divided the light from the dark and we had morning and evening, the first day. And here, those (let-there-be) light waves are speeding an original goodness to us from back in the beginning, to illuminate *this* particular, precious, present moment.

In a corner, stone masons are chipping away, fashioning their own sacred space from rock, hewing folds and edges, every angled chink of energy given lovingly to the task, calling out what has been hidden for millennia and is about to be given expression, blinking for the first time into this June sunlight.

At the opposite corner of the cloistered quadrangle, another kind of sculpture, this one in metal, by Barbara Hepworth. A famous piece of hers, '(Construction) Crucifixion' – three crosses, a moon and sun, and simple angular metal beams that let you see through the structure to what lies beyond: the lawn, the branches of the tree, the grey of flagstones. A sign explains how 'the partial openness of the work draws the cosmos into its scope and allows us to rest within it'.

Twenty minutes pass like seconds; they always seem to when you step out of the merciless beat of clock time into the expansive rhythm of the present. The body loosens; the eyes soften. Consciousness deepens; something settles.

It's time to move on – we can't sit here all day, can we? – but it's funny how, after time out, your steps are less hurried, as you slow once again to the truer pace of wisdom.

Light falls like a Constable painting

We head back through the city centre, to discover the tranquil Queen Elizabeth Gardens that provide a green pathway through to Salisbury's famous water meadows. From Crane Street bridge, we find ourselves strolling alongside the limpid waters of the River Avon again.

It is quiet, the willow trees occasionally stirred by a gentle breeze. Mums relax in the shade with their toddlers. The flower beds and the river banks are alive with hundreds of butterflies, dragonflies and damselflies. Particularly striking are the banded demoiselles with their bright metallic blue bodies. They rest from time to time on the tall purple spikes of loosestrife, the creamy white flower heads of meadowsweet and the reeds that line the river banks. The meadowsweet flowers create a fragrance that wafts through the warm air. We pause to enjoy this perfect English summer afternoon and then cross a bridge into the water meadows, heading towards the Old Mill.

It is famous as the location where John Constable painted one of his huge landscapes, 'Salisbury Cathedral from the Meadows', first exhibited in 1831. Constable became friendly with the Bishop of Salisbury's nephew John Fisher and was a

regular visitor to the city. When Constable's wife Maria died in
1828, Fisher invited his heartbroken friend to stay with him in
Salisbury and encouraged him to paint the cathedral. Despite
his grief at this sad time, Constable's resulting landscape is
suffused with light and has a rainbow as its central feature. He
considered it to be one of his finest works.

* * *

Wow. We have a print of the painting, and manage to locate
the spot from where it must have been painted. An inauspicious
little bridge entering the water meadows. Another woman
plays with her two toddlers where, below us, there is a forded
entrance into the slow-moving waters of the Avon.

And while the immediate landscape of trees has changed (the
view is obscured by many more willows which have grown
up since Constable's day), the bend in the river is undeniable,
when we hold out the print before us – as is the angle of the
cathedral spire; and suddenly we're seeing the same view as
one of the greatest painters 'saw' it, and ... it's very humbling.

And to remember, too, that this was a man who had recently
lost his wife and who must have felt a searing grief as he stood
here; and a man who was finding himself, little by little, too,
restored through his friendship with John Fisher, and through
his faith, and through studying and expressing the cathedral in
relationship to its natural surroundings.

The picture seems an exquisite – let's say sacred! – expression of the way the whole of the landscape, of which the
cathedral is a part, is sacred. In a sense, the cathedral looks
like a side-chapel within the great cathedral of creation. And
just as Constable has painted in a border collie, and horses,
and a farm worker in a carriage, and a boatman, as well as
the natural landscape, I begin to imagine Howard and myself
painted into the scene – the scene here in which we're standing
– by God; after all, each of us is a work of art, a thing of beauty
that reflects a unique facet of the divine creativity.

Of course, painters can always see more than just a landscape, and their art can inspire us, ultimately, to see more for

ourselves. I might have wandered past this spot and not for a moment truly 'seen' it; certainly not as Constable did, nor the way, in particular, he watched the light fall, as he brushed into life the glowering storm clouds to his left, the opening, freshly sun-lit, meadow to the right, and the rainbow through the centre, which spoke of the faith and the hope he could sense, despite everything.

In his book *Anam Cara*, John O'Donohue writes:

There is such an intimate connection between the way we look at things and what we actually discover. If you can learn to look at your life in a gentle, creative and adventurous way, you will be eternally surprised at what you find.

Constable, in a lecture he gave in 1844, spoke of the symbolic hope that is represented within the painting: 'I mean more than the rainbow itself. I mean dewy light and freshness, the departing shower with the exhilaration of the returning sun.'

The longest day fades from view

Our day is not quite over. There's first a refreshing stop at a pub in Whiteparish, looking out across meadows, enjoying the late afternoon sunshine, to ask ourselves, What have we learned? How might it change us? What have we loved most about it?

And to mark the closing of a very special day, we decide to head to another National Trust site, Stockbridge Down, near the small town of Stockbridge in Hampshire, to observe the sunset. It affords a perfect vantage point.

As with Pepperbox Hill, the grassland is covered with a carpet of tiny flowers and the surrounding hedgerows are overflowing with their own summer flowers, seeds and fruits plus the ever-present wild clematis scrambling over them all.

It is a still evening as we walk up the half a mile or so from the roadside to our viewing point, the silence broken only by the harsh, croaking calls of corvids: crows, jackdaws and rooks. They peck ceaselessly at the cowpats scattered across a gently sloped horizontal stretch of pristine downland, searching for beetles and grubs.

* * *

Out of left field, there's a rush of horses, 20 or so of them running wild. It's one of those moments when you remember that the image we have of nature must never be set in soft focus and stuck on a chocolate box. Hooves thunder on the hollow turf, and for a few moments we have no idea whether they're coming for us, or lost in some kind of solstice reverie of their own. Sometimes we set God in soft focus, too. But God is in those horses, a wilder, sublime kind of energy that we can't always control, and that it's important to respect.

Mercifully, they chase past – it turns out they're from a local riding school, and are enjoying some free time – and our racing pulses begin to find some rest, as we continue up the hill, jump a stile, and sit in the vertiginous west-facing field to watch the sun begin its descent, its work almost done. Hampshire stretches like a painter's canvas before us, fields softly undulating, lit by the lightest touch of touching light. What might Constable have made of this?

It's up to us, up here, to see the light.

The blues and pinks of the morning return for their reprise. The moon, rising behind us, is beaming humbly, its pure, toothpaste white cleansing the palette. A sense of deepening satisfaction arises too, as the sun falls before our eyes: we were there to witness this longest day.

Imagine if we could bring this wakefulness to the ordinary, in-between days of which our lives are mostly made up, we reflect. What difference might it make, remembering, every morning, every evening, that we gather, as humanity, within this towering cathedral of the Earth; our passing lives, the act of worship?

Activities

- Get up before dawn on the longest day (21 June) and find somewhere to observe the sunrise.
- You might even like to try the challenge of staying outside from sunrise to sunset, as a celebration of the light.
- Practise simply watching how daylight falls. It could be in a cathedral's cloisters, but likewise you can do this anywhere, of course. Simply watch it closely, bringing all of your attention and awareness to it, and let it happen.
- Find a piece of artwork or photography that represents your local area, and then go to that place to observe, through the eyes of the artist, what they have seen.
- You might, alternatively, like to go somewhere local and sketch a scene. Don't worry if you're any good at art or not – simply use the process as a meditative way of looking more closely, creatively and compassionately at your local area.
- Identify one artefact that you treasure. Contemplate that object. Consider the people it represents, or the stories behind it.
- Practise 'going with the flow' of a walk/experience rather than planning too much and/or being too analytical about it. As you go, try to 'see the sacred' all around you and within you, being awake to and aware of God's love in the midst of the everyday.
- Watch a sunset, giving thanks for what has happened during the day. You might ask, What have I learned? How have I changed? What have I loved the most?

7

July
A Truly Ancient Pathway

The Harroway, Hampshire

We can grow so quickly familiar with where we live, and with the usual paths we take, that we forget there are alternatives. Yet it's as important to see our own 'back yard' with fresh eyes as it is to travel long distances to experience new and spectacular sights. For *this*, *here*, is where we spend most of our time, and to see *this here* with renewed perspective is surely the richer challenge.

When we see a place for the first time, our senses are heightened, and we pay closer attention than usual to the hidden details – the things that we may soon end up taking for granted. In turn, this opens a window, however briefly, upon the present moment: a glimmer of awareness, during which we are more alert and alive, and ready to engage with the world around us at a deeper, soulful level.

Seeing your locality *as if* for the first time might simply involve taking a different route home from work for a change, or walking down a street in your town or village that you've never been down before. Today, Howard and I want to explore a different kind of path through our local landscape; new to us, but in fact one of the truly ancient paths in the country, which will take us through close-by stretches we have not previously explored, in an atmospheric and inspiring way.

* * *

We aspired to walk part of an ancient trackway, ideally a route used by pilgrims and not too far from home. After some digging, we came across an intriguing reference to the Harroway in Christopher Taylor's Roads and Tracks of Britain. *He describes it as prehistoric, and a link between the Pilgrims' Way from Canterbury via Guildford in Surrey to Salisbury Plain and the road on to the south west of England. In fact, it stretched all the way from Dover to Devon.*

Parts of the Harroway are sadly now under the asphalt and concrete of the A31 and A303 but a short section still remains as a green lane between the villages of Whitchurch and Oakley in Hampshire. Fortunately, it is clearly marked on the Ordnance Survey Explorer map.

So this is where Brian and I are heading for our July saunter, just after several spectacular thunderstorms, and inspired by the words of Edward Thomas (in Beautiful Wales*), that ancient ways are 'potent, magic things', on which you can 'make time as nothing' while 'meandering over many centuries'.*

On the verge

Driving up the hill north of Overton to the Harroway, we're struck by an extraordinarily colourful variety of summer flowers on the road verges: an unexpected surprise and a delightful prelude to our walk.

At the lay-by where we park, there is a sign: 'Wild Flower Verge, Hampshire County Council'. A glance at its website reveals that the Council has a joint scheme with Hampshire

Wildlife Trust to manage road verges for wildlife and to iden-
tify and protect those of particular ecological importance. It
explains:

> *Verges are often the only remaining semi-natural habitat in*
> *a farmed or urban landscape. This means they have had no*
> *artificial inputs of pesticides or fertilisers and have not been*
> *ploughed or re-seeded and can support a rich and varied*
> *range of plants.*
>
> *Many verges are remnants of ancient meadows and wood-*
> *lands still supporting some of the species that have vanished*
> *elsewhere in the countryside. This botanical diversity in turn*
> *provides a haven for insects, butterflies, small mammals and*
> *a feeding ground for birds.*

Good work, Hampshire!

Space in the margins

And what of the verges of our lives, which may be more significant than we realize?

It's tempting to make the outward appearance of life look
trimmed and neat, controlled and presentable. Yet the end
result can be like a garden with such carefully manicured lawns
that we're afraid to walk on the grass, let alone allow kids to
kick a football on it, or invite any wildlife in to make its home
there once more.

Some people like to have their religious beliefs perfectly
arranged, too. Yet it's often on the blurrier edges of life that
faith really flourishes, if given the chance. If we are willing
not to have everything we believe in its 'right' place, we can
become open to the surprise of what might emerge, like the
speckled beauty of wild summer flowers by a roadside.

* * *

'My garden is an antidote to perfectionism,' writes Jane Upchurch in her book *A Leaf Between My Toes*. 'For every blade that is trimmed, and dead flower or branch that is cut, there are a myriad others, an ever-changing interplay of life and death, of growth and decay, of beauty and chaos.

'Perhaps all is beauty,' she continues. 'Perhaps God's perfection isn't that of a smooth rose but includes the gritty soil, the falling away to fruit and fade, only to flower again in the future.

'Perhaps I don't have to be so hard on myself,' she concludes. 'I don't have to try to measure up, but can trust that if I grow my inner garden it will be a place for the spirit of God to walk.'

Walk on.

On to the ancient pathway

There is evidence that 'ridgeways' along the hills in the south of England have been regularly used by people and animals as far back as Neolithic times, over 5,000 years ago.

To the west, the Harroway passes Avebury, Stonehenge and other Bronze and Iron Age sites. It is intriguing that the main Roman road in the area, the Port Way from Silchester to Old Sarum, is a few miles north of the Harroway. Through Anglo-Saxon and medieval times, the Harroway would have been a track in constant use by local people and their animals, pilgrims on their way to Canterbury – and other travellers who wanted to avoid paying tolls, or to indulge in some poaching, or simply to lie low from the attention of landowners or magistrates in the towns and villages of the valley!

Walking the Harroway makes us more deeply aware of the very long and rich history that we share and the myriad of life stories that have been told along these lanes. If only the flints embedded in the path could speak!

* * *

I admit I'm prone to over-excitement – but for me the prospect of stepping off the tarmac country lane and on to what Howard reliably informs me is one of the oldest pathways in Britain feels electrifying.

It looks as good as it sounds, too; the way lined by squat trees which bend to create mysterious archways through which we seem to enter a timeless kind of space.

The July sunlight filters gently through leaf and branch on to the green-brown path, as it has done surely for thousands of years. Holy ground again! Just the very thought of this old path reminds me that every step through life is a gift, if we walk it attentively. And the fact that people from Neolithic times have wandered this particular way reminds me of more – that we are part of an extraordinary continuum of history.

Sadly, we now find ourselves increasingly disconnected from much of the wisdom of that continuum which was passed down almost by osmosis from generation to generation. And that's what we begin to consider as we walk. How many of us can now identify more than a handful of flowers or plants along a route like this, for example, let alone begin to advise upon which plants and berries are edible or medicinal or toxic?

I saw a TV wildlife programme about Alaska, in which an indigenous woman was interviewed. She belonged to a tribe that had lived continuously on the same land for 10,000 years. When asked how her forebears had learned to survive the often inhospitable wilds of Alaska, she explained that they had learned about the two most crucial things, food and medicine ... *from the bears*. And this wisdom has been passed from parents to children, all the way to the present.

In westernized culture we have swapped the communal fire for the TV; we have stayed in, and atomized. Walking this path in Hampshire makes us wonder what kind of people, and what kind of wisdom, from even just a handful of generations back, we might have lost touch with.

And what kind of wisdom we can pass on.

O taste and see!

The poet Robert Frost coined the phrase 'talks-walking' to describe those soulful walks he had with his friend Edward Thomas in the South Country, which yielded such abundant fruit in the form of their encouragement of each other to write poetry. Here on the old pathway, Howard and I find ourselves physically more closely in step with each other. When you're walking quietly, gently, with someone else, you can find yourself in synch – with your steps, your breathing, your very sense of being.

Perhaps that's how God likes to walk with us, too.

'We are all just walking each other home,' writes Ram Dass. What a thought. It's such a privilege, to get to 'walk' with others through life, isn't it? Think of all the souls who've helped in your home-coming. And of those you've helped, just by walking alongside.

Think of walking with God.

* * *

Simply walking without trying to get anywhere fast can help. And once we slow down, we see things we'd normally miss, such as all sorts of berries and nuts forming along the sides of the Harroway. Sloes, hazelnuts, blackberries ... Personally, I thought they 'came out' in the autumn, but if you come out yourself in the summer, you'll see them growing. Howard drops a line into our conversation about 'fruitfulness in the lanes' and it resonates. Here is literal fruitfulness, which is to be tasted and has sustained wayfarers and foragers and wildlife for millennia.

The blackberries are already ripe for the picking; at least some of them are. How delightful, tasting something again for the first time in a year. Here are gifts, scattered in the hedgerows. We haven't done anything to deserve them. They are not a reward. The Earth blesses, if we are willing to open our mouth, and our heart, to receive.

My wife once served up cheesecake for dessert, and our youngest daughter asked, 'What does it taste like, Mummy?'

Quick as a flash, my wife replied, 'The only way you'll know is if you try it!'

Betsy-Joy edged towards the outstretched spoon, popped a morsel of tangy cheesecake on her tongue, and an irresistible smile broke out across her face. '*Whooooaahhhh*!'

As the psalmist puts it, 'Taste and see ...'

The way of pilgrimage

We are walking east along the Harroway and have become immersed in a 'green tunnel' that draws our eyes along the ridge of hills towards Oakley.

The close-packed trees and shrubs on either side of the track often form ivy-covered bowers. These would have provided welcome places of shelter for travellers on stormy nights.

Some of these travellers would have been pilgrims, who, on tracks like the Harroway, were walking with particular purposes in mind: as an act of devotion to God; to seek penance for sin; to receive blessing and perhaps healing at the shrine of a saint.

For most people in medieval times, pilgrimage was an important but relatively local affair. Only those with the time and the means could undertake longer journeys to major shrines at places like Canterbury or Rome. In any event, pilgrimage was a sociable practice, with new friends made along the way and convivial overnight stays at religious houses such as Waverley Abbey near Farnham in Surrey.

In their book Sacred Britain: A Guide to the Sacred Sites and Pilgrim Routes of England, Scotland and Wales, *Martin and Nigel Palmer write:*

Exploring a sacred place involves two journeys – physical and metaphysical – running side by side. While such places are often powerful in their sense of the divine, they require something from you as well ... The encounter with the sacred in our landscape is two-way: your response is what is needed to make the encounter happen.

Your response is what's needed.

* * *

Many pilgrims will have walked the stretch of the Harroway we're on, because it also connects to Winchester, the ancient capital of Wessex (and of England, once King Alfred had unified the country by the end of his reign in 899).

Winchester became an especially popular place of pilgrimage thanks to St Swithun, who was once its bishop, and who now provides a well-known meteorological legend associated with July – as well as plenty of soulful food for thought about our own lives and legacy. As the traditional rhyme puts it:

> St Swithun's day if thou dost rain
> For forty days it will remain.
> St Swithun's day if thou be fair
> For forty days 'twill rain na mair.

St Swithun's day falls on 15 July, and it's said that if it rains on that day, it will then rain for 40 days continuously. It's a legend that is local to Howard and myself (and there will be legends, stories and lore that are specific to your own area; stories that were once passed down by word of mouth or perhaps through song).

Swithun was known for his kindness and humility. He eschewed the company of the rich – despite his powerful ecclesiastical role as bishop, and his role as a trusted adviser to King Egbert – in favour of helping the poor. In fact, he is reputed to have walked from place to place in bare feet as a sign of humility.

On his deathbed in 862, Swithun asked to be buried not in a grand and showy grave, which would have been his right, but outside the old minster in Winchester, in a humble grave.

However, as his reputation grew in death, more and more pilgrims came to visit Winchester, believing that his bones had healing properties. And so the monks created an elaborate shrine for him inside the cathedral and moved his remains there, partly in reverence, though partly, without doubt, to capitalize on all the pilgrim footfall!

On the day that he was moved, there were ferocious storms and there followed weeks of continuous rain, signalling his great displeasure, according to the legend – which is why we're warned that if it rains on 15 July, it will rain for 40 days.

While there's no scientific truth to the idea, the weather patterns at this time of the year do have a habit both of shifting, then of sticking for several weeks, due to the seasonal movement in the jetstream. So there may be something in it, after all.

But Swithun's example more helpfully reminds us to consider the nature of our life's work, and whether we are doing things in order to be remembered, or simply for the sake of doing them (in service and love).

Swithun reminds me of a line from the prophet Micah: 'Act justly, love mercy, walk humbly'. It's simple, memorable counsel for walking the path of life, literally and metaphorically.

'To open my eyes and behold'

We reach a T-junction and a grassy side-turning that heads south towards the upper reaches of the Test Valley. A signpost in the hedge simply says 'Byway'. We don't know where it leads, but we're tempted just to explore.

Lao Tzu once said, 'A good traveller has no fixed plans, and is not intent on arriving.' There's a freedom to such movement, which puts the focus upon what we encounter and learn along the route; how we grow and change; and who we find ourselves changing with.

So we savour the sight of a red kite, which accompanies us for a good stretch of our walk, swooping low to the fields, then soaring high for a predatory vantage with hardly a flap of its wings. The kite, as we watch, seems in flow with its environment.

We realize that flow is a word that keeps recurring for us. It's sometimes spoken of as a serene state of being and doing without having to over-think or over-strive. The author Mihaly Csikszentmihalyi (in his book *Flow*) puts it like this: 'Flow is being completely involved in an activity for its own sake. The ego falls away. Time flies. Every action, movement, and thought follows inevitably from the previous one, like playing jazz.' Watch any bird of prey on the wing and it will surely remind you of that flow. You can enter a similar state during walking, of course. Just try not to think too hard about it ...

* * *

We are also stopped in our tracks by the magical sight of a hare – and then another – and then another! – at close quarters; one pair lollops up the path, all ears and ponderous limbs, while another suddenly legs it across the nearby field.

It's quite unusual to see a hare today. We hadn't set out to see one, specifically – but had we not set out, we wouldn't have seen it either.

In fact, we've rarely stepped out into the countryside without being surprised and overjoyed by the sight of something unfamiliar. The American writer Annie Dillard describes the joy of unexpectedly seeing muskrats, and observes: 'They show me ... what a prize it is simply to open my eyes and behold.'

And it's in the *peripheral* vision that we can often notice an unexpected movement in nature. In fact, it can pay dividends just to stand still, and relax your eyes, and 'let the world in' instead of trying to focus on any one particular detail. It's easier to spot a subtle movement in this way, something you might otherwise have missed. You become more keenly aware of what's happening there on the edges of what you usually see.

It's a principle to take into life itself, too – to watch for what's occurring on the edges, the fringes, and in the places you least expect it.

* * *

Hares have long been a source of fascination for artists, writers and country people who have embedded tales of the hare in folklore. Aesop's fable of the hare and the tortoise dates back to the sixth century BC and helped to create the maxim that 'keeping on wins the race'. Albrecht Durer's watercolour of a young hare, painted in 1502, is regarded as an early master-piece of observational art. The 'mad' March Hare at the Mad Hatter's tea party was immortalized in Lewis Carroll's Alice's Adventures in Wonderland.

In the countryside, hares lead an often solitary, nocturnal life, and stories of them gazing at the moon were probably behind an association with the pagan moon goddess Eostre and a belief in the magical powers of the creature. The sight of a hare was also thought by some to foretell bad luck, if not disaster, especially if it crossed your path.

But we choose to see our sighting as a blessing! And much more positively, the early nature writer Richard Jefferies, in Wild Life in a Southern County (1878), describes the 'boxing' of hares in springtime:

> *They stand on their hind legs (which are very long) like a dog taught to beg, and strike with the forepads as if boxing ... round and round they go like a couple waltzing; now one giving ground and then the other, the fore-legs striking all the while with marvellous rapidity. Presently they pause – it is to recover breath only; and 'time' being up, to work they go again with renewed energy, dancing round and round, till the observer cannot choose but smile.*

He's right. Even though we don't see the boxing match, we cannot choose but smile.

* * *

The fabled speed of the hare puts us in mind of the 'flow' we can experience at a faster pace, too. After all, while much of the focus of contemplative spirituality is about slowing down or stopping completely to reconnect, aren't there times when it is simply wonderful to go *fast*? When we catch sight of a dog in full flow soon after, expressing an absolute creaturely joy through its racing body and its bounding presence, we feel that joy, too. This is freedom of movement, full-throttle, and contagious!

As a runner myself, I can sometimes experience flow when I'm opening up in the countryside, and I'm reminded of the Olympian Eric Liddell's famous line, immortalized in the film *Chariots of Fire*: 'When I run, I feel God's pleasure.' Perhaps the secret is to find the kind of relaxed poise and artistry that comes through the practice and dedication of an athlete or a dancer who becomes beautifully adept at moving well, at speed. Isn't it good, to accelerate, with grace, at times, especially when it comes with the overflowing joy of the Creator coursing through your veins.

After the storm

As the path leads us from the edge of fields and into a pocket of woodland, Howard is particularly taken by the smell of the earth, which is so vividly fresh after a series of heavy storms, following a very hot spell, immediately prior to our walk.

It gets us talking about the nature of storms (such a significant feature of summer) and their place in our lives. One of the recent storms had woken me during the night with the loudest thunder-crash I can remember (and it had made me thankful that I have never lived in a war zone).

I had got up out of bed to watch the lightning after the initial shocking boom, and I realized, several minutes after, that my heart was still racing and I was physically shaking. Most of us are sheltered from the immediate threats and challenges of nature, yet a thunderstorm can still hook our instincts at a primal level. And that part of us deep, deep within which is perhaps most natural knows that we are not lords and masters of the world we survey but, at best, invited guests within it: and should act as any invited guest would like to act, with respect, and even reverence, for the place in which we find ourselves.

* * *

The particular smell when rain begins to fall on dry earth is surely as distinctive as the scent of freshly mown grass or the mustiness of woods on a damp November day.

It has a name, 'petrichor', derived from two Greek words: petra meaning 'stone' and ichor the fluid that flows in the veins of the gods in Greek mythology. What a beautiful image: a life force emerging through the stones of the earth.

The scientific explanation for the smell was first published in the prestigious scientific journal Nature in 1964 by two Australian researchers, Isabel Bear and Richard Thomas. Certain plants exude oils during dry periods that are absorbed by clay-based soils and rocks. During rain, these oils are released into the air, along with another compound produced by bacteria in wet soil. It is the combination of these chemical substances that creates the distinctive smell. Lightning during thunderstorms may add the specific smell of ozone to the mix.

The immense energy generated by lightning also combines nitrogen with oxygen in the atmosphere, creating nitrogen oxides which dissolve in the rain as nitrates. In this way, rain falling during thunderstorms becomes a source of natural fertilizer for plants. Some scientists believe that humans appreciate the rain scent because our ancestors relied on rainy weather after long dry periods for survival. Certainly we were appreciating the re-greening of the countryside after the storms as the plants absorbed life-sustaining water.

And if scientific explanations leave you feeling the need for something more imaginative, here is a short poem by Nadine Swan, called 'Pluviophile' (rain-lover):

when everyone
clings to their umbrellas
avoids puddles
and walks on damp earth

you will find her
dancing in the rain

The Eternal Now

Sometimes, as you are walking, you might happen upon a moment of stillness – or did it happen upon you? – that speaks with particular eloquence. A moment of clarity, we might call it, or presence – in which somehow everything seems more vivid, connected.

We find ourselves upon a wider stretch of pathway, a secluded spot where the track bends around an area of woodland, and there we pause without talking, and all feels still. There are no traces of the contemporary world; no masts or pylons, no cars or buses, no houses or shops. We could have been standing in the same spot at any point in the preceding centuries, and the chances are it would have looked hardly different. It's a powerful moment, which silences the two of us.

When we find ourselves somewhere that is essentially timeless, save for the seasonal adjustments in the foliage in the hedgerows and on the trees, the place can call to somewhere timeless in us, if we listen.

My children sometimes get frightened by the idea of 'eternity', the thought that time simply never stops (What will we do in heaven for all that time?). A different way to see it, perhaps, is in terms of the fullness of this moment, which transcends time. Here is the 'Eternal Now', if you like. Pure presence. And once we become attuned to it, it's possible to sense it within even the most fleeting of contexts, and to bring something of its timeless presence to the rushing, racing world around us.

We can offer assured and loving glimpses of the Eternal Now to those whom we meet, too – those who may be anxiously looking back to what's already past, or nervously forward to what might not even happen ...

I will bring myself back to this moment, here on this path, when next I feel stretched to breaking, myself, within the push and pull of twenty-first-century life.

The butterflies

Sunny, still days in July and August are the best times to see adult butterflies on the wing. It's not ideal weather today and we are not experts but, as we walk the Harroway, we are pleased to identify several different varieties: speckled wood, holly blue, red admiral, small white and possibly a clouded yellow. The latter species has been a regular migrant from Europe in the summer. It may now be resident, as winters get warmer.

They'll come into your back garden, particularly if you have their favourite food plants, such as buddleia, marigolds and lavender. But good locations for butterflies in the countryside are chalk downland and the wide tracks (or rides) through deciduous woodland. Most butterflies add colour to summertime and they have a wonderful variety of names: Duke of Burgundy, purple emperor, silver-studded blue, painted lady, green-veined white ...

To find out more about the 59 species of butterflies that breed in Britain have a look at the Butterfly Conservation website: www.butterfly-conservation.org. Sadly, the organization's leaflet, 'Gardening for Butterflies and Moths', includes these alarming words about the threat to our butterflies:

Butterflies are far less common now than they were 50 years ago and you don't have to look hard to find out why. Flower meadows filled with butterflies were once commonplace, but now they are little more than a memory. Since the 1940s, 97% of these meadows have been destroyed together with much downland, ancient woodland and peat bogs. Even common butterflies have lost out as hedges and field boundaries rich in wild flowers and grasses have gone under the plough.

If there is even a small green space around your house, you can make an important contribution to butterfly conservation by growing the right shrubs and flowers. If you have a larger garden, consider leaving some unkempt edges; plant a few packets of wild flower seed and keep the nettles. Nettles are the main food plant for the caterpillars of four of our most beautiful butterflies: the comma, red admiral, small tortoise-shell and peacock.

* * *

The Big Butterfly Count is a nationwide survey which happens annually in July and August in the UK – the world's largest butterfly survey, in fact. And it's one simple way not just of helping the natural world by tracking the (dwindling) numbers of butterflies in Britain, but also of being helped, ourselves, in the process.

The idea, simply, is to sit for fifteen minutes in the garden or in a park or woodland, and to pay attention, and count butterflies – which can be a delightful, meditative way, within our restless culture, of learning again to 'be still', as the psalmist says.

I'm reminded of Simone Weil, who once wrote that prayer is 'absolutely unmixed attention' – and watching butterflies has to be one great way of being prayerfully present in a non-religious manner.

Jesus referred his followers directly to nature, surely for good reason. 'Consider the lilies,' he said. 'Look at the birds of the air.' We can learn so much about our own place within the natural world because we are part of it, not set apart *from* it – a truth we so often forget.

I loved watching butterflies as a child. It's a powerful memory. And when my son was about to have a heart operation a few years back, I went out with him that same summer morning to look for butterflies. We were both scared. Not only did it keep us calm, but it gave us a way of reflecting together on the nature of the transformation he was to undergo – the movement from one stage of life into the bright but as yet unknown colours of another.

* * *

We might also use the sight of a butterfly in summertime as an opportunity to express lament for the species we are losing, or have lost. The author Mark Jerome (as quoted in Francis Weller's extraordinary book on grief, *The Wild Edge of Sorrow*) writes:

> Each extinction is a unique voice silenced in a universal conversation of which we ourselves are only one participant. When the tiny wings of the Xerces blue butterfly ceased to flutter, our world grew quieter by a whisper and duller by a hue ...

There's really no time like this present, to tune back in to the whispering of nature, and to each unique voice within the glorious but lamentably diminishing whole.

Ambling homewards

It's late in the afternoon, the weather is clearing, and we reflect on the nature of walking the path.

For Robert MacFarlane, in his inspiring book *The Old Ways: A Journey on Foot*, there's a fascinating link between walking and *learning*. He traces the etymology of these two words back through Old English and Proto-Germanic to conclude that 'to learn' means, at root, 'to follow a track'.

He's so right. We keep walking, and we keep learning. And each path we find ourselves upon becomes part of the greater pilgrimage. We walk the path of life, and the path seems to come alive itself as we set careful feet upon it.

When the Victorian novelist and historian Walter Besant read the observations of the celebrated nature writer Richard Jefferies, he exclaimed: 'Why, we must have been blind all our lives; here were the most wonderful things possible going on under our very noses, but we saw them not.'

Mercifully, it's never too late, we surmise, to start to treasure that which was hidden in plain sight on this journey all along. Treasures on the road that calls us home.

Activities

- Find a new route to walk locally and research the 'place' before you go.
- Walking slowly, look for a flower that you don't recognize, identify it and share the knowledge with a friend (photograph the flower, don't pick it).
- Leave a patch of your garden to grow more wildly. Loosen your control on one part of your life that you have previously been tempted to micro-manage!
- Stand in the rain. Without an umbrella. Take joy in the rainfall! Give thanks for something you might not usually welcome which is nevertheless a blessing.
- Search for local legends, perhaps by visiting the local museum or church. If there is the story of a saint among them, ask yourself in what ways they are an example to us today (perhaps through their acts of kindness, justice, mercy or humility).
- Take part in the next Big Butterfly Count and learn more about butterflies, the decline of many species and their conservation: www.butterfly-conservation.org.
- Use 'soft eyes' in nature. Stand outside, nice and still, for a few minutes, and relax your gaze. Let the world in through your eyes in a relaxed way, instead of focusing on any one thing in particular. This is a relaxing and meditative process. Become aware of your peripheral vision, and sense the world around you. Keep watch, in particular, for any unexpected wildlife such as hares!
- Go for a run, if you are able, and 'feel God's pleasure' at the strength, the pace, the endurance, the poise when you are 'opening up' and increasing your speed.

8

August
The Story of My Heart

A visit to Coate Farm, Swindon, home of Richard Jefferies, and a walk upon the Ridgeway to Uffington

It is enough to lie on the sward in the shadow of green boughs, to listen to the songs of summer, to drink in the sunlight, the air, the flowers, the sky, the beauty of all. Or upon the hilltops to watch the white clouds rising over the curved hill-lines, their shadows descending the slope … in-drawing the life of the earth and the sun.
(Richard Jefferies, *The Story of My Heart*)

As our severance from Nature widens, so Richard Jefferies' messages increase in importance. Jefferies [is] the most deeply spiritual of our Nature writers and the first and truest nature conservationist. His message is simple: in Nature we truly belong.

(Matthew Oates, writer, broadcaster and former naturalist with the National Trust, writing in the visitor guide for the Richard Jeffries Museum)

* * *

Richard Jefferies, who lived from 1848 to 1887, is not a name that most people would recognize, yet he's widely regarded as a founding father of modern nature writing, alongside Gilbert White, W. H. Hudson and Edward Thomas.

One of Jefferies' best-known books, Wild Life in a Southern County *(1878), is based on walks from his home at Coate into the surrounding countryside, up on to the Wiltshire Downs and along the ancient path known as the Ridgeway. At the time, Coate was a small village outside Swindon, but it has now been absorbed by the town.*

Jefferies' writing, which I remember finding on my grand-father's bookshelves, was a source of inspiration for me as a biologist and for my lifelong interest in natural history. One could learn so much from his acute powers of observation and his deep knowledge of the local landscape. He gained these qualities by walking in the area where he lived, often slowly and with regular pauses for reflection.

Brian and I have chosen to start our August walk by visit-ing his birthplace at Coate Farm, which is now the Richard Jefferies Museum. It's nestled beside a dual carriageway, next to a pub and opposite a garage – but still surrounded by resid-ual countryside in the form of Coate Water Country Park.

The farmhouse itself is an uneven combination of an orig-inal tiny thatched cottage joined to a more substantial nineteenth-century stone building. It retains many of the fittings and furnishings from Jefferies' time. Mike, a volunteer with the Museum Trust, is there to welcome us with a cup of tea, takes us around the house and gardens and shares the history and plans for the future of this special place.

Seeking inspiration

It is fascinating to see where an inspirational person has lived or worked or walked (or all three, in Jefferies' case). There's a whiff of lingering presence here, for sure, especially in the bedroom-cum-study with its humble wooden desk; the museum is a work in progress, and it feels as if Jefferies could return home at any moment. Mike gives us the run of the place, and we step through the same doorways, and stare out of the same windows, and try to imagine how someone like Jefferies could see the ordinary world with such fresh, wondering eyes.

After all, he didn't live in some magical kingdom; he lived somewhere near Swindon. And he didn't necessarily have what you might call great raw materials, as a nature writer: no steepling mountains, no vast plains, no great lakes, no grand canyons. No volcanoes or tornadoes or deserts or glaciers. Just ordinary fields, hedges, hilltops, rivers, to touch his heart.

He seems to have combined keen observation with soulful response, and, long before mindfulness became popular in the West, he was writing exuberantly, ecstatically, of the soul-deep connections we can experience when we step outside to behold, and to be *within*, nature. You could say that he bequeathed an extraordinary gift: by putting the language of soul into nature, and the language of nature into soul.

'Moving up the sweet short turf,' he writes, about climbing a local hill, 'at every step my heart seemed to obtain a wider horizon of feeling; with every inhalation of rich, pure air, a deeper desire ...'

His inspiration is here both metaphorical and literal; the breathing of the air is life-giving in every way, and this is what's so wonderful about Jefferies: the physical and the soulful are indivisible. 'By the time I had reached the summit,' he recalls in *The Story of My Heart,* 'I had entirely forgotten the petty circumstances and the annoyances of existence. I felt myself, myself.'

* * *

It's intriguing and electrifying to Howard and me that Richard Jefferies channels his own response to nature into what he calls 'prayer': 'The grasshoppers called and leaped, the greenfinches sang, the blackbirds happily fluted, all the air hummed with life. I was plunged deep in existence, and with all that existence I *prayed*,' he says.

His 'prayer' is not religious, as such, but mystical. It's a yielding, through the body, of our human desire for communion and belonging.

And anyone can do it – just lie down in a field with your arms outstretched, look up to the sky, notice your senses and be present. Witness this moment. Feel the Earth support your back and your being.

I remember leading a retreat in London, once. As part of the day, I took a small group into Green Park (one of London's most excellent green spaces), and encouraged the participants simply to lie down, and to look up. Ben was there, a psychotherapist who'd been working with children in war-torn areas of the world. He was tired, and understandably close to burnout. We reflected on all sorts of beautiful ideas that day, and went to some magical places, yet for Ben the simplest sense of being supported, lifted by the Earth within that quiet moment in Green Park, was what mattered. It endured, a sense of restoration and reconnection that you simply can't manufacture.

Such an experience is akin to what we might call contemplative spirituality, which offers a form of prayer beyond mere words, through just being here, intentionally, consciously, vividly, thankfully – giving yourself to the moment, as well as (if you like) to God.

We so often see prayer as a means of asking for things we need. But if we turn it around, to offer our self most fully within any given moment, fully present, alert, compassionate, awakened, then we become the prayer, and – who knows? – perhaps even the answer to it.

The path less taken

Coate Farm had been falling into disrepair until it was taken over by a group of committed, hardworking and visionary volunteers. One of their projects involved clearing the walled garden from a jungle of brambles so that vegetable and flower beds could be re-established. Mike mentions with pride that pupils from a special school often arrive with troubled expressions on their faces but leave smiling, even if it has been pouring with rain. Gardening, like being in the countryside, can be therapeutic.

Refreshed and raring to go, we then head towards the Vale of the White Horse, to walk where Jefferies walked, and to experience August on another of England's very old tracks, the Ridgeway. It runs from Goring Gap on the River Thames to Salisbury Plain, and is one of a handful of prehistoric trackways in Britain dating back thousands of years – along with the Harroway, the Icknield Way (a northerly extension of the Ridgeway) and the 'South and North Downs' Ridgeways'.

It is only a short drive along a quiet lane that connects Swindon with Wantage, winding upwards through the villages of Hinton Parva, Bishopstone (where a lone heron patrols the village pond), Idstone with its little thatched cottages, Ashbury, Knighton and Woolstone to the National Trust car park at Whitehorse Hill. Just ten miles as the crow flies from the centre of Swindon and we are deep in countryside. You never need travel far to experience the calming influence of green spaces.

A short walk up the hill accompanied by another red kite and we are alone, heading west along the Ridgeway in search of an intriguingly named local landmark, Wayland's Smithy. It is a hilltop tomb or 'long barrow'. We are following in the footsteps of people from the Stone Age, Neolithic farmers who came up here to bury their dead.

* * *

As we set out on foot we notice, soon after the car park disappears from view behind us, that we can't see another soul, nor sign of civilization. Just the red kite rising, a serene reminder that we are not entirely alone. And the path: a white chalky snake of a path, and truly ancient; cajoled by gentle banks of grass and nettles on either side, and sandy, hardier grasses swaying like summer, chin high.

We are sauntering into a space that seems happily less populous, even as the vista, with its orderly rows of sweetcorn to the left, and its brittling swathes of barley to the right, opens up before us and spills out all over Jefferies' country.

Onwards we walk. And there is a rhythm to foot-fall when you settle in to a longer stroll. As we've found time and again, the need for talking subtly subsides and, in the widening gaps between words, you experience more of the unspoken presence of a companion. It's a rare but good thing to find an assured solitude within company that lets you just *be* with each other.

I can imagine heartbeats aligning, as well as feet. It's another glimpse of communion. Sometimes the richest kind of settling-in happens on the go; a sense of stillness in motion.

The August sun warms not just the skin but the heart, and a pair of red admiral butterflies offer up their own display of unfrenzied companionship, gliding in from out of shot, settling on the purple heads of a tufty gang of thistles; opening their wings wide to the day, and drinking deep, as we pause, too, to drink all this in.

Pure nectar.

The ultimate gallery above

As humans, we spend most of our lives looking straight ahead, and there may be good reasons for this. From the earliest times, the first sight of a stranger's face gave a clue about whether or not the natives were likely to be friendly. Once we became more mobile, we needed to look ahead to be safe when riding a horse or driving a chariot, carriage or car. Our eyes are also slightly sunken into the skull, with the ridge of the eyebrows above and the cheekbones below, making it require a bit more effort to look up or look down. But when walking in the countryside, making that effort brings rich rewards.

Our walk along the Ridgeway on a beautiful August day gives us good reason to look up. We are already well above the surrounding countryside but our field of vision becomes dominated by the sky and the rich array of clouds that stretch to the far horizon. Richard Hamblyn in his book Extraordinary Clouds *writes:*

> *Clouds present us with an ongoing visual spectacle that transforms the sky into a constantly changing, mood-altering display of light, shade, volume and colour – 'the ultimate art gallery above' as nature writer Ralph Waldo Emerson described it. A vast outdoor exhibition space that is open to everyone.*

A space that has inspired so many of the great artists, of course, including Turner, Constable and the Impressionists. And the sky really is a massive three-dimensional space, with flat stratus clouds below 5,000 feet (1,500 m) and bubbly cumulus clouds rising to 10,000 feet (3,000 m). On fine days, wispy cirrus clouds of ice crystals can often be seen very high up, above 30,000 feet (9,000 m). Giant cumulo-nimbus clouds tower from near the ground to above 30,000 feet (9,000 m) and warn of an approaching storm.

* * *

We can see the whole billowy array, today, from high up here on the Ridgeway, painting washing-day whites and glowering greys across the infinity of August-blue sky.

The clouds aren't just impressive to see, however. They remind us of a different *way* of seeing, if we let them. It's one thing to step back and admire the view and judge it to be sublime or otherwise; but as you step out along a path such as the Ridgeway, it's as if you're stepping into the view itself.

After all, as Gavin Pretor-Pinney, founder of the Cloud Appreciation Society, reminds us, we don't live beneath the sky, but 'within it'. We are creatures, he says, who inhabit 'this vast ocean of air'.

So when we stop to breathe the air, we breathe the sky. And we can do this anywhere; in fact, it's perhaps even more significant when all around us seems like glass and bricks and mortar.

As Jefferies puts it in *The Amateur Poacher*, 'Let us get out of these indoor narrow modern days ... into the sunlight and the pure wind. A something that the ancients called divine can be found and felt there still.'

There is sky in the soul.

* * *

Talking of the ancients, hidden in a circle of beech trees just off the Ridgeway, but with magnificent views through the trees northwards to the surrounding Oxfordshire countryside, we come upon Wayland's Smithy.

It's an impressive Neolithic long barrow, 185 feet (56 m) long and 43 feet (13 m) wide, with four towering standing stones at the sealed entrance to the tomb. The earth is raised several feet above the tomb, and covered with lush turf. As we ascend the five stone steps to this little plateau, we find it's the perfect place to stop for a rest, too.

Archaeologists have proposed that this site was built in two different phases, a timber-chambered oval barrow constructed around 3550 BC and then a stone-chambered long barrow built 50 to 100 years later. The Neolithic period in British history heralded a gradual but widespread change in lifestyle, from nomadic tribes of hunter-gatherers to more settled farming communities.

Wayland's Smithy is one of many prehistoric sites associated with Wayland or Wolund, a Germanic smith-god. The name was probably applied to the site by the Saxons who settled in the area about 4,000 years after the tomb was built. The first documented use of the name is in a Saxon charter dated AD 955.

We have our lunch sitting on the long barrow, enjoying the late summer sunshine. We then lie on our backs, watch the clouds for a while, and dream ...

* * *

It truly is one of those rare but unforgettable moments when all goes completely still, and you find yourself flat on your back on the grass, watching not just the clouds but the clouds of birds passing overhead – the swallows and swifts, in particular, icons of the season; and you know that here you are, deep within the heart of summer. Here is rest.

In fact, I'm minded of the words of the farmer and poet Wendell Berry, who writes in his collection *Leavings* of 'the maker's joy', in which we, too, may 'come to rest'. Is that what it is, when we sense that summery ease of heart within nature, and we don't know where it comes from?

That drowsy sense of timelessness comes washing over us again, helped by the presence of the ancient burial site that connects *this* summer moment with the thousands that have come, and gone, in the time since the people beneath the warm turf at our backs were laid to rest. The brightest beech leaves above, fluorescent in the sun, cast a kind of spell inviting you to blur your eyes and fall upwards into the welcoming swathes of tree-greens and sky-blues.

Jefferies knew this spot well, though he had another favourite long-barrow site closer to his home in Coate. Year after year, he notes, 'the blue butterflies had visited the mound, the thyme had flowered, the wind sighed in the grass ... Nothing has to come; it is now. Now is eternity ... Here this moment, by this tumulus, on earth, now; I exist in it.'

And you sense that this day could be any day in August or all the days there have ever been.

* * *

In 1738 Francis Wise, an Oxford academic and antiquarian, recorded a belief held about this site in local folklore, referring to it as 'Wayland Smith' rather than 'Wayland's Smithy'. According to the account of local people:

> [A]t this place lived formerly an invisible Smith, and if a traveller's horse had lost a shoe upon the road, he had no more to do than to bring the horse to this place with a piece of money, and leaving both there for some little time, he might come again and find the money gone, but the horse new shod.

Visitors to Wayland's Smithy have continued to deposit coins in the cracks of the stones around the tomb, no doubt as some sort of 'good luck' charm – but not to leave their horses! Eventually, English Heritage, the organization that now manages the site, removed reference to the coin deposition custom from the information panel. Perhaps this decision has reduced the overall impact of a visit to Wayland's Smithy for, as the folklorist Ceri Houlbrook notes, 'the depositing of coins contributes to the ritual narrative of the site'.

How interesting, the pull of simple ritual acts – whether leaving coins at Wayland's Smithy, or flowers at a roadside shrine, or the lighting of a candle in a cathedral. Small acts that express something of our search for meaning, for story, for connection.

To see what we could see

We take a slow, observant walk back along the Ridgeway towards Whitehorse Hill to observe more closely what is left of summer's flora and fauna. There is plenty of fruitful greenery along the hedges and verges of the track but, among the verdure, we can still find 20 different plants still in flower. It is a colourful scene, with the purples of willowherb, burdock, thistles and knapweed; the red of herb-Robert; the whites of bindweed and yarrow; the yellows of wild mignonette, hawkbit, nipplewort and toadflax; the sky blue of scabious and, on the slopes of Whitehorse Hill itself, delicate, nodding harebells.

We pause to watch several bumblebees diving deep into the

thistle flowers in search of nectar, but it is the old dead stalks and seed heads of hogweed that turn out to be the best places to find invertebrates. On one such remnant of an earlier flowering, we identify a magnificent longhorn beetle, with greatly extended black and blue striped antennae, as well as a ladybird, a comma butterfly and plenty of snails. Snails of several types are common on chalk downland as calcium, a vital component of their shells, is readily available.

Richard Jefferies, in Round About a Great Estate, has this to say about snails:

> Some of the folk ate snails, the common brown snail found in the hedges. The method of cooking is to place the snail in its shell on the bar of a [fire] grate, like a chestnut. And well-educated people have been known, even in these days, to use the snail as an external medicine for weakly children: rubbed into the back or limb, the substance of the snail is believed to possess strengthening virtues.

We see more red admirals that keep settling on the path just in front of us. They are known as the 'people friendly' butterfly as a result of their habit of resting on humans. There are also brownish coloured skippers, our smallest butterfly. The name derives from their short, darting flight from flower to flower.

Halfway along the track between Wayland's Smithy and Whitehorse Hill, there is a curious signpost in the hedge with three arms marked 'footpath'. Two of the arms make sense, pointing east and west along the Ridgeway, but the third points directly north into the middle of a large field of maize. The farmer has helpfully cut a neat two-metre-wide path through the tall crop. At the signpost, we chat briefly to a mother and her young daughter. They had just followed this path for a quarter of a mile but, seeing no end in sight, retreated to the Ridgeway. However, their diversion was worthwhile as the girl stood captivated by the texture of the long iridescent, silky hairs from the maize cob she was holding in her hand. It was good to see a young person experiencing the beauty of a natural object, found unexpectedly and by walking slowly and observantly.

This odd footpath through the field of maize, apparently leading nowhere, prompts me to have another look at the Ordnance Survey Explorer map. Between the villages of Ashbury and Woolstone, a distance of only two miles, there are ten tracks and public footpaths that provide access from the nearby villages and the lane from Swindon to Wantage up on to the Ridgeway. The path through the maize is one of them.

It is likely that many of the lanes, tracks and footpaths still marked on Ordnance Survey maps have been public rights of way for centuries, if not millennia. These ten points of access, along a relatively short distance, suggest that the Ridgeway has been a busy thoroughfare in regular use by drovers, local people, travellers and now walkers, from the first Neolithic farmers more than 5,000 years ago to the present day.

* * *

The sight of the woman and her child exploring the country paths certainly inspires us. The girl was so clearly absorbed in the process, and wisdom and inspiration were being shared back and forth between the two. It was, in a sense, an unusual sight, grace-filled and gentle. I'm immediately grateful for my own friendship with Howard, and grateful to receive his wisdom and inspiration, which I hope, in turn, to pass on.

And we love the idea that Richard Jefferies passed on inspiration. His children's books, *Wood Magic* and *Bevis*, didn't just inspire the children who read them, but also inspired twentieth-century authors such as Arthur Ransome (*Swallows and Amazons*) and Henry Williamson (*Tarka the Otter*) to write about adventures in the countryside. And his work has influenced and inspired a host of present-day nature writers, whose books, in turn, are helping us to reconnect with nature.

You may never realize what you trigger by being willing to explore with others, and to be curious, and to share your curiosity. In your own lifetime, you may not have the recognition; you may not get awards, or even be thanked. Yet if you throw yourself in with wonder and grace, it's likely that the fruits of your own growth will turn to seed, like the myriad seeds that are forming along the hedgerows, and that will soon be blown, carried, dropped to the ground, deposited or buried ...

A planting.

* * *

Towards the top of Whitehorse Hill, we cross a stile and make a final steep ascent to Uffington Castle. The whole hilltop, including the castle, is a Site of Special Scientific Interest, as it is one of the few remaining unploughed grasslands along the chalk escarpment in Oxfordshire. This type of grassland has a particularly rich, and sometimes rare, variety of plants and animals, providing the foundations for an unusual ecosystem.

The 'castle' is, in fact, an Iron Age hill fort, now an extensive open area of land enclosed by a single, well-preserved bank and ditch. In the centuries before the Romans came to Britain, it would have been the relatively secure place where the local Iron Age farmers retreated with their families when they were under attack from hostile tribes. The panoramic views to the far horizon from the castle are breath-taking.

* * *

Then a moment of utter surprise and delight, as a skylark suddenly lifts off from the ground almost next to us, a lark ascending, lifted as if by the fullness of its song. And fullness is probably the word – the skylark, almost incredibly, can sing over 200 separate notes or 'consonants' *per second.*

The widening view opens up a widening sense of connection. There's that undeniable link between the body and the soul when we are out and walking, and especially when we are marching up a hill. You have to put your back into it, as well as your heart.

I make a mental note to remember this: so often life seems 'uphill', and the up-ness gets me down. But this physical climb brings a smile to our faces. It feels inherently good, somehow; perhaps it's because we're tracing the contours of the earth, and with them, we're part of this Earth again, muscle and sinew and feet and hands and sweat and aches all reconnecting to what, deep down, they know so well.

There's usually an extra little bit to climb, just when you think you've made it to the top ... But that's OK, too: a reminder that being only part-way there is a fundamental part of the process. It's perfectly all right that you have not reached your destination, even if you wish you had.

And what is it about looking to the horizon, when finally you get there? This great visual reward for reaching the top. It seems to cleanse the eyes. We gain perspective. We are a small, and mercifully insignificant, part of greatness.

As we sit here at the top, I do so with a man who has experienced suffering. People with life experience have a different viewpoint – so often, they are better able to see the bigger picture; to put the pettiness of minor worries into perspective.

A hill lifts you a little nearer to the clouds, a little higher into the sky around you, lifts your spirits and soul, whispers '*Look!*' and lets you look down, for a change, upon flying birds, lets you trace the patterns of fields, helps you to imagine what it might be like to have wings yourself and fly.

* * *

On the northern slope of the hilltop is the famous White Horse, a figure carved into the turf in several separate parts and extending for 360 feet (110 m). The latest archaeological evidence has dated the horse to the late Bronze Age (1000–800 BC). It may have been a tribal symbol, carved by the same people that built Uffington Castle. Similar horse-like symbols appear on Iron Age and Anglo-Saxon coins. In addition to the design of coins, the Uffington White Horse has been the inspiration for substantial creativity down through the ages: in art, literature, music and the carving of white horses on other hillsides. In 2003, the Guardian *newspaper (4 May) commented that, for more than 3,000 years, the Uffington White Horse has been jealously guarded as a masterpiece of minimalist art.*

But why was it carved? The carving process must have been

long and arduous as the figure is 'drawn' with trenches up to one metre deep, filled with crushed chalk. Where did the local people find the resources to create it when life was short and tools were limited? Perhaps they used slave labour from captured tribes. Perhaps it was a deeply religious symbol, designed to placate pagan gods – and therefore worth the effort. Perhaps it is significant that the whole horse can only be seen clearly from a distance or from the heavens. There are lots of unanswered questions, but they all help to create the intriguing mystery of the Uffington White Horse.

From a more practical perspective, during World War Two, the figure was covered with turf and hedge trimmings to prevent German pilots from using it as a navigation aid during bombing raids. In normal times and without cleaning, the figure would quickly become obscured by the natural growth of vegetation, and there is a long history of regular 'scouring'. Until the late nineteenth century, the horse was scoured every seven years as part of a more general local fair held on the hill. Here is Francis Wise again, writing in 1736: 'the ceremony of scouring the Horse, from time immemorial, has been solemnized by a numerous concourse of people from all the villages roundabout.'

This periodic scouring continues, now organized by the National Trust. On 'chalking day' volunteers with hammers, buckets of chalk and pads kneel beside the figure, smashing the chalk to a paste and whitening the paths cut in the grass centimetre by centimetre. Only masochists or monks need apply!

* * *

It's late afternoon, and as we gaze downwards at this magnificent chalky work of art – the horse resting to the right across a flank of the downs that tapers from where we sit – its head seems to gaze back up at us, its penalty-spot eye for ever fixed, open. Who chose to put that eye precisely *there*? And how did they get it so right, so measured, without a helicopter view to help?

It's impossible not to feel stirred again – at the thought that creativity has always coursed through us humans, from the ancients who first saw these hills as their canvas, to us sitting here within today's glimpse of the Eternal Now. As naturally as a bird sings or a cloud forms, creativity flows within us all. And as we yield to our own God-given createdness, we can yield, too, to its ever-present creativity.

We can't all leave something indelibly marked on a backdrop such as these Wiltshire downs for thousands of years to come, of course. But what we can offer back to the landscape, to the moment, to the people around us, to the world of which we are a part, is our full and true selves: whether stomping the path exuberantly, or climbing the hill with heart and perseverance, or falling flat on our backs in slumberous mid-afternoon satisfaction, like a prayer.

By now, the sun is easing itself down from the heights of this dreamy day; the shadows lengthen across the billiard-green slopes of Uffington Hill, as a line of people, humble as ants, descend towards the car park.

Simple pleasures await: for us, a resting of the legs, a mug of tea from the flask, a slice of flapjack, and new passages to weave into the story of our hearts.

Activities

- Explore a more natural/practical way of praying, using fewer words. Simply try lying down on a lawn or in a field or park, and feel your body supported by the Earth. Let your whole self relax deeply into the moment, and feel a part of creation.
- Watch the clouds, and give yourself permission to do nothing *but* watch them for a short period. Remember that we are 'creatures who inhabit this vast ocean of air', and breathe it in, as if it's God's love.
- Practise looking down, sideways and up rather than straight ahead and, in particular, spend regular time during the day and on clear nights looking at the sky.

- Look for summer flowers and insects. Try to find something you can't immediately identify, and work out what it is. Expand your range of knowledge!
- Try to release some creativity, like the skylark, by doing something creative that you've almost been too scared to attempt, for fear of failure. Just give it a go.
- Get involved with something like the White Horse clean-up – there are all sorts of local projects to help with, through the Wildlife Trusts or organizations such as the National Trust.
- Try reading something by Richard Jefferies. Or else why not revisit an old nature favourite, such as *Tarka the Otter* or *Swallows and Amazons*?

9

September
Real and Colourful,
Fruitful and Whole

An autumnal walk through the town of Romsey

Autumn. It can creep up on you like a mist, with so many swirling emotions: from the heart-warming invitation to wrap up cosily and kick through piles of leaves like a kid, to that melancholic fret of time passing; of summer days slipping our grasp.

It's too early for autumn 'proper' – but the horse chestnut trees are already turning, as they like to in early September, from green to rusty russet red, like a warning; and there's dew falling in the mornings, be-jewelling all the cobwebs …

'*Nothing lasts for ever*,' autumn seems to whisper.

And it's all too pertinent for us this year, as we very nearly lost Howard to heart failure since last month's walk (there we were, reflecting on the 'story of my heart'). But with emergency surgery, he's edged his way back from the brink, and today we both feel keenly alive to the intimate presence of death in life, and life in death.

* * *

This is the second time in my life I have had to face my own mortality. The first followed my family's involvement in a serious road accident nearly 40 years ago, in which Beth, our seven-year-old daughter, died and I was seriously injured. I was told after nearly three months in hospital that, without pioneering plastic surgery, I might have died from infected wounds.

Last year, and to my surprise, I was informed by a doctor that I had a heart murmur. I was offered the opportunity to have a new 'keyhole' approach to the repair that avoided the trauma and slow recovery of open-heart surgery, and bounced back from the operation quickly. However, during the summer we realized that something was wrong. Heart failure followed rapidly and I had an emergency admission to hospital for open-heart surgery.

That evening, my wife and daughters were called in to be told that I might not survive the night. Mercifully, I did and I'm now left to reflect on the second significant experience of facing my own mortality.

Dear Beth had only seven years of life; I have had 74. Facing into and working through suffering (and it comes to us in many different forms) seems to be an essential part of growing up, emotionally and spiritually. Perhaps it's an uncomfortable truth we have to accept that life is a mix of good times and bad times, happiness and tears, life and death. Without one, we would not know the other.

* * *

It's true, isn't it? We tend to see life and death as polar opposites. But intriguingly, and perhaps even comfortingly, autumn's own mysterious, unsettling beauty is found right *within* its tangle of seeming opposites – beauty and decay, light and dark, fruitfulness and withering – which aren't necessarily opposites at all, but part of what Parker J. Palmer calls a 'hidden wholeness'. He writes:

> If I try to 'make' a life that defies the diminishments of autumn, the life I end with will be artificial at best, and utterly colourless as well. But when I yield to the endless interplay of living and dying, dying and living, the life I am given will be real and colourful, fruitful and whole.

It makes our own sense of loss, or grief, or disintegration, no easier to cope with, sadly – but it does help us, perhaps, to be more present, even welcoming, to the pain as well as the pleasure, to the darkness as well as the light. Instead of trying to push away our hurt, it's possible to incorporate it, with wisdom and honesty, into the 'hidden wholeness' of our life, and thus not have to deny it, or forever run scared from it.

That's what I've seen Howard do. So I know it can be done.

The mundane and maligned

Given that I have to take it easier, we choose to stay close to home for this saunter – which makes it the perfect opportunity to explore the 'natural' spaces within a town, and, in particular, my own home town of Romsey.

Towns and cities have a surprising range of wildlife and, if you live in the suburbs or near an urban green space, you can often see many species without even leaving the house: birds and butterflies, slugs and snails, spiders and smaller insects. In Romsey we've a canal, a river, flooded meadows and plenty of garden ponds, all of which provide ideal habitats for dragonflies, frogs, toads, slow-worms and grass snakes.

A family of hedgehogs often wanders past at dusk. And a good neighbour of mine, Mr Bunney, who (despite his name) used to own a ferret, tells me that an old fox regularly pads through the neighbourhood in the early hours.

We have another resident, too, which I confess I've been rude about in the past: the much-maligned pigeon. It is, after all, often a portly, over-sexed, scruffy creature that gathers like a nuisance in large numbers, especially if there is food around.

And yet, descended from the wild rock dove, domestic pigeons have played a valiant part alongside us humans. They have such a strong homing instinct, and can fly so fast at high altitude, that around 250,000 homing pigeons were used during World War Two.

Thirty-two pigeons, in fact, were awarded the Dickin Medal, the highest decoration for valour given to animals. One of those, a pigeon named 'Cher Ami', lost both a foot and an eye yet successfully delivered a message that saved a large number of American infantrymen.

* * *

There's often deep goodness to be found in what's seemingly mundane and maligned. Jesus spoke of how God cares for every unremarkable sparrow. So while we might be tempted, consciously or not, to disregard those who seem unattractive to us – including ourselves – God, meanwhile, continues actively to love all creation.

And if God does, perhaps so can we. In fact, we don't need to track down an area of outstanding natural beauty to learn to love the natural world more deeply and pro-actively. Take a step outside and look at an ordinary pigeon through the eyes of God, for a start.

Or step *inside*, and look in the mirror, through those same eyes.

* * *

As we set off along his road, past a line of typically trim suburban semis, with their neat hedges and fences, Howard reminds me to put a 'hedgehog hole' in the bottom of my own garden fence. Autumn should be a time in which activity in our gardens peaks, and hedgehogs love to roam around one-

and-a-half miles (2 km) each night. Yet we're blocking wildlife from flowing through our urban spaces with all the fences we put up, and I realize it's true – no living thing could squeeze under mine!

And all the while we're busy building and protecting our own little private kingdoms, it's not just the hedgehogs we'll 'keep out' of our lives, if we're not careful. Certainly someone like me, an introvert to the core, could afford to make a few more of their borders permeable, and welcoming to the community of all God's creatures, humans included.

* * *

Soon, Howard and I are walking along a ring-road of sorts, typically non-descript except for silvery flashes shimmering through the thick vegetation that borders the road. We cross to look, and there's a broad expanse of water, complete with a mysterious line of bare poplar trees rising up from below its surface. The trees are bereft of greenery, aside from great balls of mistletoe which look like Christmas baubles.

A cormorant has chosen its flight path directly above us, and makes its final descent to the water. It's only then that I notice hundreds of birds lined up on the exposed branches.

* * *

This is a 'good news' story for the local environment: Fishlake Meadows is an area of about 60 hectares, originally drained for grazing by continuous pumping. Twenty years ago, the pumps were turned off and the area flooded (hence the trees rising from the water), allowing for the return of a burgeoning variety of birds, insects, mammals and other wildlife. Water voles and otters are now well established and ospreys regularly pause here to feed during their seasonal migration.

A developer acquired the land and applied for permission to build houses on some paddocks adjoining. It was finally granted, with the proviso that the flooded area be handed back

*to the local authority, along with a substantial grant, to manage
the area as a nature reserve, enabling the long-term protection
of a precious wetland.*

Green corridors

*The east side of Fishlake Meadows is bounded by a disused
barge canal, which opened in 1794 and (with its adjoining footpath) continues into Romsey itself, connecting gardens, parks
and other green spaces and thus creating a 'green corridor' into
the centre of the town.*

*Passages like these are vital for wildlife: they connect popula-
tions that are otherwise separated by roads and buildings. This
kind of joined-up-ness allows for the exchange of individuals
between different groups, which increases genetic diversity. It
also helps to facilitate the re-establishment of populations that
have been reduced or eliminated by catastrophes such as fire
or disease.*

*Ironically, we need green corridors not just in our towns, but
also in the countryside, which is increasingly being stripped of
its hedges and its biodiversity. The conversion of old railway
tracks into footpaths and cycle paths, and the installation of
green 'wildlife bridges' as part of major road improvements,
are slowly beginning to create more green corridors.*

* * *

As we wander the canal towards the centre of town, clusters
of viburnum berries sprinkle the predominantly green hedges
with vivid red bursts. Blackberries cling a little higher up, just
evading Howard's eager grasp. Acorns provide a crunch under
foot, their once green jackets crinkling, cracking, as they evoke
that 'endless interplay' between life and death.

Howard points out water-mint, and the delicate blues of
forget-me-not sprays, their shy yellow centres offering nostal-
gic glimpses of the late summer that is nestling within this early
autumn. A gust dislodges a helicopter squadron of hornbeam

seeds, which land across the gravel path and on the surface of the water.

The canal's green corridor causes us to consider the 'chunks' of time we set aside personally to find rest or play or a more soulful connection with life. Days like today, which we can see more as a rare treat than as part of a regular, life-giving rhythm.

How much value are they, if they're just occasional one-offs, that don't join up? What small rituals and practices might help to reconnect these greener patches in our lives?

Howard tells me that a little copse of trees, stuck in the middle of a huge farmed field, is of very limited use to wildlife because it is so cut off … And that seems like a powerful metaphor for the pockets of soulful rest we grant ourselves, if they only ever happen in fragments, in isolation.

Under the spreading chestnut tree

In town, we rest for a while under a large, dome-shaped horse chestnut beside the library. It's one of my favourite trees in Romsey. In late spring, the crown of the tree is covered with showy white flowers, enhanced by delicate yellow and pink patches towards the base of the petals. It's always a magnificent sight. And in September, as Brian laments, the leaves are already turning brown and beginning to fall.

The horse chestnut grows wild in a relatively small area of northern Greece and Albania. It was introduced to the United Kingdom early in the seventeenth century and has now become established as a favourite on village greens and in the streets and parks of our towns and cities. Unlike the sweet chestnut, which was probably brought here by the Romans, the horse chestnut is not commonly found in deciduous woodland – it's very much a 'townie'.

But why 'horse' in the tree's name? It may be a warning, as conkers contain a substance that is toxic to horses. Another explanation relates to the horse-shoe-shaped scars left on the branches and twigs when the leaves fall off. Each scar contains seven 'nails', the points at which conducting tissues once connected the leaf with the main stem of the tree.

* * *

It's a soulful exercise to identify a single tree and to return there each season. The horse chestnut is ideal, with its elegant flowers in spring, its great cooling spread of foliage in summer, its vividly turning leaves in autumn, even its horse-shoe scars in winter.

Around our feet, a few green husks are already fallen and splitting to reveal that gleaming brown smile of the conker inside. They always looked so shiny and new to us, as kids, just like the shiny and new school shoes with which we would crack into them.

I'm cheered that my own children experience that same raw excitement today, and in that sense the horse chestnut is a great tree to help any of us connect to nature, as it's been part of our consciousness from such an early age.

If you look carefully at the tree, you can also see signs of the sticky bud that will flower next spring. Already here, then, as summer turns to autumn, there are also signs of the spring that's to come.

Howard, pulling out his trusty notebook from his kit bag, reads a few choice words from John O'Donohue's *To Bless the Space Between Us*, explaining how the transition from summer to autumn is slow, and begins unseen during the previous season:

Nature insists on taking its time. Everything is prepared. Nothing is rushed. The rhythm of emergence is a gradual, slow beat; always inching its way forward ... Change arrives in nature when time has ripened. There are no jagged transitions or crude discontinuities. This accounts for the sureness with which one season succeeds another.

* * *

From a scientific perspective, the transition to autumn that we are observing in the horse chestnut – the change in colour and the falling of leaves; the ripening of the fruit – is controlled by plant hormones.

One group of hormones, the auxins, begins to decline during the summer, resulting in the breakdown of the green pigment chlorophyll, thus exposing the reds, oranges and yellows of other leaf pigments. The reduction in auxins also stimulates the growth of a corky layer between the leaves and the stem of a plant, eventually cutting off the supply of essential nutrients and leading to leaf fall.

At the same time another plant hormone, the gas ethylene, stimulates the ripening of fruit. These hormonal changes are triggered by a gradual reduction in the temperature and the amount of light as the days shorten. The physiology of plants, despite their sedentary lifestyle, can be as complex and fascinating as that of animals.

* * *

Across the way, set against an old Romsey wall, plump apples are beginning to bend on the branch, ruddy like outdoorsy cheeks, while a stream of Virginia creeper, blood red for the season, pours over and down the brick like lava. As we stop to enjoy some evening primrose growing in the hedge, a blackbird lands, picks off a berry, swallows it and flies off. Sparrows flit through the hedgerows too, snacking cheerfully on the berries, eating on the go. God loves them all.

Making space in community

Romsey is a 'transition town', one of a number around the country committed to building a low-carbon community. With permission from Network Rail, volunteers have installed raised beds to grow vegetables on a bank beside the path up to the station. They have also planted fruit trees in one of our parks and invited people visiting the area to pick (without charge) the apples, pears and plums as they ripen.

Passing through one of the town centre car parks, we cross a bridge over a stream and enter the delightful garden of King John's House with its adjoining Tudor cottage. The house, the oldest in the town, was once part of a large medieval complex and dates from the thirteenth century. During the 1990s, its overgrown garden was bought by the local council and lovingly restored by another group of volunteers. Part of the garden has plants selected because they would have been known before 1700; it also includes small areas of spring meadow, summer meadow, waterside, herbs and flowers. The remainder has been designed as a Victorian garden. The garden of King John's House is now a haven for wildlife and a sanctuary for people living and working locally who want a few moments of quiet and relaxation, with the possibility of drinking their tea from a bone china cup!

* * *

It really is a haven. There's something sumptuous about 'stopping' within the sanctuary of a set-aside space, when all around you is noise and activity. Simple benches nestle into lovingly trimmed hedges, and arches support climbing roses. People come here who don't have gardens. They're actively involved in creating an inspiring space in the community.

So this is where Howard and I choose to enter some intentional stillness. We bring our attention to our breathing, relax the body, settle into the space, and pause to be. On a day like today, how can we not pause to notice the heart, beating; and the gift of life coursing through our veins? Today is all we have, and we receive the gift with sincerity, and a smile.

* * *

Close by, there's a tree, and it bears great bulbous yellowy green fruit, which I simply don't recognize. One of the gardeners helps me: it's quince, and part of the pre-1700s garden. Such an unusual sight, but one that would have been familiar in centuries past.

As we move to go, we pause by one of the many small streams that ripple like arteries through Romsey, toward the River Test. With a loud plop, a red, ripened apple falls from an overhanging bough and splashes into the clear water. It joins several other huge specimens that are bobbing downstream as we watch.

There is abundance in autumn; fruitfulness, ripeness, profligacy.

* * *

Just across the road from King John's House, we enter the precincts of Romsey Abbey. Originally founded in the tenth century as a Benedictine nunnery, it has been, since the time of Henry VIII, the parish church. It is a grand old building, still home to a thriving Christian community that serves the locality.

The triangle of grass between the abbey and the vicarage is dominated by another of my favourite trees: a very large oak. We're here to search for galls. Galls are growths on the oak's leaves caused by tiny parasitic wasps. They range in size from the appropriately named cherry gall to the much smaller but also well-described silk-button gall. The wasp larvae feed on the tissue of the gall, eventually emerging as a new generation of adults.

Why the fascination with oak galls? For me, it's their association with the early manufacture of ink. Iron gall ink was the standard writing and drawing ink in Europe from the fifth to the nineteenth centuries. It was traditionally prepared by adding an iron salt to a solution of tannic acid and binding the mixture with gum arabic. Oak galls were a common source of the tannic acid.

A well-prepared ink would gradually darken to an intense purplish black. The resulting marks would adhere firmly to parchment or vellum. Unlike india ink, they could not be erased by rubbing or washing but only by actually scraping a thin layer from the writing surface.

* * *

Some time ago, a friend gave me a special fountain pen, and I was so touched that I have subsequently tried to write notes of thanks and appreciation with it, in order to pass on the blessing I felt in receiving it.

In an age of e-mail bombardment and hastily dashed-off texts, a handwritten note, in ink, from a good pen, has the capacity to last so much longer in the hand and the heart. Composed.

There's something about the connection between hand and pen, pen and paper, that helps us to make a mark upon someone else's life in a well-crafted way.

Handwriting is a process that can help to release our deeper-down thoughts, too. It always strikes me, when I write in my journal, just how rich the process of a hand-written reflection can be.

So how lovely, to bestow the riches of that process on someone you'd love to thank, for who they are, or for what they do, or for how they've travelled alongside you. You may not know quite what to write for them, until you put pen to paper. That's part of the joy: to learn, yourself, what lies within, and to let it flow.

Walking the labyrinth

Across the road from the abbey is the Catholic community of the Daughters of Wisdom. I want to take Brian here not only because there's a colourful, well-tended garden, but also to walk its labyrinth. As a project to celebrate the millennium in 2000, the community decided to re-develop a walled garden as a grass and brick-paved labyrinth which is open to anyone who would like to walk it, free of charge.

Unlike a maze, which is designed to get you lost, a labyrinth takes you on a winding journey from the outside to the centre and back, and serves as a spiritual practice. This labyrinth is based upon the design of the oldest surviving labyrinth in the world, which dates from around 1220 and can be found (and walked) in Chartres Cathedral, France.

* * *

I adore labyrinths, and this one is a beauty! It's another sanctuary, a public space set aside for reflection and stillness, within that wonderful walled garden, and bordered by another of Romsey's streams.

This labyrinth is a brick path, which curves through a grass lawn. As with any labyrinth, you can trust the path, despite its twists, to take you right into the centre, and back again. And it leads you into a richer sense of space, as you go. What an oasis, then: an ancient spiritual practice serving those of us seeking to find a path through the unique challenges of twenty-first-century life.

The idea is to walk slowly, and to notice what you notice along the way. You might reflect on where you've come from, where you're going to, and what lies at the centre of life for you. I'm reminded of some words by the theologian Frederick Buechner:

Listen to your life. See it for the fathomless mystery it is. In the boredom and pain of it, no less than in the excitement and gladness: touch, taste, smell your way to the holy and hidden heart of it, because in the last analysis all moments are key moments, and life itself is grace.

* * *

For me personally, today's labyrinth helps to symbolize the path that runs through all the places Howard and I have walked so far – as well as the deeper spiritual connections we've made along the way.

It's fascinating to notice what bubbles up from within, when you walk a labyrinth. The mind settles, allowing your soul the space it needs to be heard. Mine whispers how grateful I am for my travelling companion – walking a few yards ahead of me there – and his safety and health, and for his heart, which is good.

I'm not sure what I'd have done, had I lost him. But as I watch him continue along the path, I'm also more painfully aware that he has walked graciously with grief for decades, and in a sense we must all learn to walk that way.

Not all of us, mercifully, will have to face tragedy; nevertheless, loss is inevitable, however much we would rather pretend that it's not. Surely that's why autumn snags us, year upon year. The leaves that are green *will* turn to brown. Yet when we're able to accept that times of loss will be inevitable, as Francis Weller counsels in *The Wild Edge of Sorrow*, we become better able 'to cultivate the art of living well, of metabolizing suffering into something beautiful and ultimately sacred'.

Sacred indeed. On one level, this is a simple and ordinary walk through town with a mate. And yet it's also nothing of the kind. 'Where there is sorrow,' wrote Oscar Wilde, 'there is holy ground.'

Park life

Our own path then continues onwards towards the town's park, another place for community to gather.

Romsey's War Memorial Park is quintessentially English with its bandstand, bowling green and tennis courts, together with its well-tended flower beds and a tributary of the River Test forming the eastern boundary. The latter is the setting for the quirky 'mayor's duck race', held annually in July.

The park is an expansive, delightful green space only ten minutes' walk from the centre, and has several features that help to remind the community of its more painful past.

Not far from the war memorial stands a relatively new and moving sculpture of a life-sized horse and soldier. It was unveiled by the Princess Royal in 2015 as a reminder of the massive Remount Camp, located just outside Romsey during World War One. At the camp, 120,000 horses and mules were prepared for war service – and few returned. A memorial, if you like, to the bittersweet nature of the relationship we seem to have established with all God's creatures.

* * *

Dragonflies fizz and flit, toddlers totter, and bright purple vibernum stands to attention around the ornate iron bandstand attracting a pleasingly plentiful community of bees. A mug of tea from the community café refreshes body and soul. We thank God for simple pleasures.

There is space for childhood memories to surface again; I remember a park at Hastings we used to visit when I was very small, watching the squirrels, and eating ice creams. That one had a boating lake, too, and an aviary. Sacred public space.

Four elderly ladies huddle for shelter from some friendly passing drizzle under a tree, walking sticks, flasks and sandwiches to the ready. A snapshot of people just passing the time of day. Annie Dillard once wrote in *Pilgrim at Tinker Creek*, 'Spend the afternoon. You can't take it with you.' And in this moment, she is absolutely right.

A man in pink shorts and his little boy feed the ducks. The boy looks like his dad. Surely this sort of moment is repeated through generations, timelessly. They seem lost within it, and within it they are very much found.

The smell of cut grass evokes memories of the start of the summer. A twinge of pain. Is this the last such whiff of the passing season? Breathe it deep. Mixed within it, as we stop to notice, is the uniquely cool smell of fresh running water from the tributary.

The pale warmth of the waning September sun breaks through and blesses each of us there, old and young, with equal kindness, asking nothing in return. Such selfless love as this, remarks the poet Daniel Ladinsky, 'lights the whole sky'.

Finding flow

From the park, a narrow footpath takes us only a few hundred metres to Sadler's Mill on the main River Test, where we'll complete our saunter. By now we have walked right across Romsey from the northern to the southern edge of the town. The mill was first recorded in the sixteenth century, rebuilt by Lord Palmerston in 1747 and last used for milling corn in 1932.

The crystal clear waters of the Test rush under the mill in several channels and a salmon 'leap' allows the migrating fish to make their way up river to spawn. The exquisite setting of the mill brings an immediate 'wow' from visitors when they see it for the first time. The Test flows on downstream passing Broadlands, the former home of Lord Palmerston and latterly Lord Mountbatten. Willows overhang the river, trout are resting between patches of bright green weed, and meadows skirt the river to the south.

* * *

We watch swathes of lime-green eel-grass sway within the water, mirroring the weeping willow above which bends towards the river, a picture of flow in almost suspended animation. So we pause one final time. The intentional act of pausing to watch a river flow, or eel-grass sway, or a tree bend, can help us to find our own sense of flow, if we let it.

You might not notice an immediate recalibration; yet in the days to come, you can find yourself in greater synchronicity with the world around you, and begin to notice small gifts of serendipity, moments of epiphany and reconnection, which tend to flow to us and through us, as a result.

Poetry in motion

As we've walked through Romsey, there have been a number of stone and metal plaques set in the pavement or on walls and inscribed with short pieces of poetry. Howard tells me that local residents were invited to submit poems in the late nineties, which were used, alongside the work of established poets, to create a trail around Romsey titled 'Poetry in Motion'.

Here is one of the quotations selected from William Wordsworth's free-flowing creativity: 'For I have learned to look on nature, not as in the hour of thoughtless youth, but hearing oftentimes the still, sad music of humanity.'

What inspiration, to see public places less blighted with advertising posters than blessed with lines of poetry.

As we head back to Howard's house, our hearts gently full, my thoughts turn to the words of another poet, Keats. 'Season of mists and mellow fruitfulness,' he wrote, so famously, 'Close bosom-friend of the maturing sun ...'

It's upon us, autumn. There's no denying it now. We'll soon have the equinox once more, and that delicate moment of balance, before we're tilted so very gently towards the shorter days and longer nights. There's a nip in the air, but this evening we're grateful for the many textures of life – and for the natural poetry of what's to come.

Activities

- How can you make your home and garden more wildlife friendly? Cut a hedgehog hole in the bottom of your fence, for starters!
- You might like to use a walk along a canal, or a converted railway line or other green corridor, to reflect on the rhythm of your own life, and in particular on the flow between your rest and activity, your input and output. Think about the kind of spaces you create in your average day/week to join up your 'down-time'/meditating time and to refresh yourself physically, mentally, emotionally, 'spiritually'.
- Don't forget the challenge (from February) of selecting a tree that you can return to throughout the seasons. Spend some

time there, getting to know it, by drawing it, sitting with it, returning to it, noticing.

- Revive the practice of handwriting with a fountain pen and send a beautiful card with encouraging words to a friend or someone in need, from time to time – or maybe try this for the first time!

- Try to locate and walk a labyrinth. But if not, just try a slow walk of awareness along any familiar route, and see the place again through fresh eyes. Offer your own steps as an expression of prayerful appreciation for the path you are walking, and for those who walk through life with you. And look, with love, for the natural world, of which you are part.

- If you could create some space in your weekly schedule, consider volunteering with a local project, particularly a project that is designed to improve a green space.

- Find out more about the 'Poetry in Motion' trail from either the website for Test Valley Borough Council or the Tourist Information Office in Romsey. See if you could get a group together in your own community to do something similar that captures and puts on public display the good things about the 'spirit' of the place where you live.

10

October
An Ode to Autumn

In the footsteps of John Keats, in the countryside around Winchester

Season of mists and mellow fruitfulness,
Close bosom-friend of the maturing sun ...

Straddling the end of October and the start of November is a trio of special days: All Hallows' E'en, All Saints' Day and All Souls' Day. These overlay the pre-Christian celebration of Samhain, at which the ancients marked the midpoint between the equinox and the winter solstice; bonfires were lit to mark the dying of the light.

Today, here on All Hallows E'en, we're walking with a group that has gathered on the green of the cathedral grounds in Winchester, for a saunter that will follow in the footsteps of John Keats. The 23-year-old wrote his sublime ode 'To

Autumn' in the dying days of 1819, having spent that summer and autumn in Winchester, hoping to convalesce from the ill health (tuberculosis, it turned out) that was tragically to kill him within a year and a half. Coincidentally, he was born on this day, 31 October, in 1795.

As the early afternoon sun filters through a grand old copper beech above us, and a cluster of tourists pass by, a curate from the cathedral wanders over to issue a chance blessing upon our walk. We're a diverse group – among us, a businessman who's hot off the red-eye flight from Jedda, a local academic, a CEO, an artist and a vicar ... We're all a bit disoriented in our own ways, and this is a perfect way to find ourselves back in step with more natural rhythms.

We'll wander out from the city into the water meadows where Keats took a daily constitutional, along the banks of the glassy River Itchen, up and over a hill called St Catherine's (to walk an ancient labyrinth), and back in time for cathedral evensong.

After our blessing, we begin to head off – but, turning the corner of the cathedral, we immediately find ourselves captivated by a shimmering lime tree; its green and yellow leaves appearing, from a distance, like bells gently ringing. We're so struck – awe-struck – at the way this tree simultaneously stands proud yet humble against the blue sky that we pause to give it our full attention. After all, there's no rush, and this is what we're here for.

Already, it feels like a divine moment – which is as it should be, if the former warden of Iona Abbey, John Philip Newell, is to be believed. 'The matter of life', he writes in *Christ of the Celts*,

> comes forth directly from the womb of God's being. The glory of the sun rising in the east is the glory of God shining on us now and now and now. The whiteness of the moon, the wildness of the wind, the moisture of the ... earth is the glow and wildness and moistness of God now. It is the very stuff of God's being, of which we and creation are composed.

It's no surprise that a sense of awe gives rise to wonder and then gratitude, as we stand there.

And if John Philip Newell is right, then it stands to reason that we humans are the stuff of God's being, too. To quote his paraphrase of Julian of Norwich, 'We are not just made by God, but made *of* God.' Sometimes it takes finding beauty in nature to discover the very beauty of our *own* nature. There's every reason, then, to stand both proud and humble, like this tree. So we stand some more, before slowly moving on.

Sacred space, both inside and out

The 'maturing sun' creates long shadows of the old trees as we walk onwards across the cathedral close, before diverting to ascend a steep flight of wooden steps to St Swithun-upon-Kings Gate – a tiny church, first recorded in 1264 and restricted to a hidden space directly above the old city gate, in stark contrast to the massive cathedral only a short distance away.

St Swithun's is thought to be the inspiration for St Cuthbert's Church in Anthony Trollope's novel The Warden *(1855). It is still in regular use, and is bedecked with flowers on each windowsill. 'We hope you find peace with us,' says a welcoming sign. And we do.*

Brian suggests that we let this precious, simple space help to create some space within us, too, as we settle in and sit quietly for a few minutes. A delicious hush descends, and he asks us to imagine that our inner life contains this kind of uncluttered and inspiring sanctuary within. It's a calming and soul-stirring prospect.

And after a good pause, we imagine what it would be like to create a sense of this space around us, through our presence; a space into which others may step, to draw breath and to find rest.

Mellow fruitfulness

Walking slowly out into the light, and mindful of carrying that spaciousness with us, we continue along College Street (which can't have changed much in hundreds of years) before pausing on a patch of lawn, opposite an old yellow town house. Number 8 College Street is where Jane Austen spent her last few weeks in the summer of 1817, before she died of a mysterious illness, aged 41. She was buried at a humble ceremony at the cathedral, early in the morning, in the presence of only four mourners.

A huge Magnolia grandiflora is shedding its golden and coppery leaves behind us, almost mournfully. An Indian bean tree, or Catalpa, shares its flamboyant presence alongside, with its large, pale green leaves, and long, dangling seed pods.

The house provides a poignant reminder that we can be touched personally and significantly by creative people such as Jane Austen who have dared to explore and express life artistically in their own unique way. We owe a debt to those who often lived without much money or recognition in their own lifetime, but who stayed true to their calling.

For a few moments, we share with each other the works of cultural creativity that have shaped us – from pop songs to paintings to poetry. It's good, from time to time, to revisit them, to remember how they helped us to grow, to ripen and mature.

* * *

Jane Austen finished her novel *Persuasion* in 1816, and in it she describes the season of autumn as 'the view of the last smiles of the year upon the tawny leaves and withered hedges'. She then observes, so truly, that it's a 'season which has drawn from every poet worthy of being read some attempt at description, or some lines of feeling'.

I'm sure that autumn stirs our creativity because the human soul recognizes something, deep within this season, that resonates universally with the ebb and flow of our own being within God's creation.

It's so moving to think that, a mere two years after her untimely passing, John Keats was walking past this very spot, surely with no idea that Jane had died in the first-floor room above with the bay window. All the while, autumn was indeed drawing from the poet 'some attempt at description, some lines of feeling', which would, it turns out, become one of the most important artistic works of the Romantic period.

It's the right moment for our group, then, to turn to his ode 'To Autumn', to read it aloud, and to see the world afresh – this world *here* – through the poet's eyes.

Season of mists and mellow fruitfulness,
    Close bosom-friend of the maturing sun;
Conspiring with him how to load and bless
    With fruit the vines that round the thatch-eves run;
To bend with apples the moss'd cottage-trees,
    And fill all fruit with ripeness to the core;
      To swell the gourd, and plump the hazel shells
    With a sweet kernel; to set budding more,
And still more, later flowers for the bees,
Until they think warm days will never cease,
    For summer has o'er-brimm'd their clammy cells.

Who hath not seen thee oft amid thy store?
    Sometimes whoever seeks abroad may find
Thee sitting careless on a granary floor,
    Thy hair soft-lifted by the winnowing wind;
Or on a half-reap'd furrow sound asleep,
    Drows'd with the fume of poppies, while thy hook
      Spares the next swath and all its twined flowers:
And sometimes like a gleaner thou dost keep
    Steady thy laden head across a brook;
    Or by a cyder-press, with patient look,
      Thou watchest the last oozings hours by hours.

Where are the songs of spring? Ay, Where are they?
    Think not of them, thou hast thy music too,—

While barred clouds bloom the soft-dying day,
    And touch the stubble-plains with rosy hue;
Then in a wailful choir the small gnats mourn
    Among the river sallows, borne aloft
        Or sinking as the light wind lives or dies;
And full-grown lambs loud bleat from hilly bourn;
    Hedge-crickets sing; and now with treble soft
    The red-breast whistles from a garden-croft;
        And gathering swallows twitter in the skies.

* * *

Great poetry is not always easy to decipher, and rewards repeated, careful reading; but it's sometimes enough to notice a word or phrase that especially resonates, or an image or metaphor that captures your attention. As Keats takes us through his sublime autumnal flow of ripening, reaping, gleaning, pressing, and 'soft-dying', we each, in our group, notice different things – the swollen abundance, the sense of rest and drowsiness, the oozings, the unique music of the season ... But our attention turns in particular to 'mellow fruitfulness', and 'ripeness to the core'. It's a feature of autumn that we often neglect, tending (as we do) to focus more on the falling leaves than the prospect of harvest.

The theme of fruitfulness resonates at different levels, and happily it provides a contrasting measure to the driven and egotistical way we often view 'success'. You may not consider yourself to be successful, but no doubt you've borne fruit.

The Bible offers suggestions for the kind of 'fruits of the Spirit' we can grow through our lives: love, joy, peace, patience, kindness, goodness, faithfulness, gentleness and self-control. Each has its own taste, its zing, its fragrance; each will ripen in its own time, and disperse seeds in different ways.

Summoning childhood

As we continue reflectively onwards, we find ourselves sauntering past a row of poplar trees. The sweet, musty smell of their
fallen leaves triggers a delightful flashback for me, to my grandmother's home in north London at the end of World War Two.
Her next-door neighbour's garden was dominated by several
large poplars, and as a small boy, I would help to rake up the
fallen leaves as they carpeted my grandmother's lawn.

Autumn is evocative in so many ways, but it seems, in particular, to release memories of childhood – just try kicking
through leaves with abandon! Brian challenges us, as we go,
to 'set the child within us free' to help us rediscover something
more, or forgotten, about what autumn means.

It's a reminder for me, too, that today's children may need
our help to create their own powerful memories of engaging
with this season, and with nature itself.

The signs are concerning. Despite the proven connection
between natural play and wellbeing, for example, words such
as 'acorn', 'buttercup' and 'conker' have, in recent years, been
dropped from the Oxford Junior Dictionary, to be replaced
by words in more popular usage such as 'attachment', 'blog'
and 'chatroom'. This has sparked an outcry from well-known
children's authors such as Michael Morpurgo, as well as nature
writers such as Helen Macdonald and Robert Macfarlane, who
collectively wrote, in an open letter to the publishers: 'The
Oxford Dictionaries have a rightful authority and a leading
place in cultural life. We believe the OJD ... should help to
shape children's understanding of the world, not just to mirror
its trends.'

Words let us name things – from emotions to birds, plants
and animals. Without those words, it's much harder to care for,
love, or – ultimately – save them. Robert Macfarlane's recent,
beautiful picture book The Lost Words is an artistic response
to the loss of certain words and experiences from childhood,
with his own poetic writing about such living things as ivy,
goldfinches and skylarks exquisitely illustrated by the artist
Jackie Morris. An organized campaign is under way to get

*copies of this wonderful book into as many primary schools
as possible, to help children find the vocabulary to talk, once
more, about some of the things we adults took for granted in
our own childhoods.*

Watching for the kingfisher

'Kingfisher' is on the list of words that have been dropped from
the *Oxford Junior Dictionary*. As we continue out from the
city to the edge of the water meadows, we pause by a bridge to
watch the pristine water of the River Itchen flow beneath us,
and Esther, the chief executive among us, tells me how much
she'd love to encounter a kingfisher. She has never seen one.
I have to admit that it always stirs my soul to catch an unexpected glimpse of flashing kingfisher blue – because for me it
evokes something of the exhilarating and wild nature of God's
presence.

So we agree to keep watch as we go, and I'm reminded of
Ann Lewin's poignant poem about prayer, called 'Watching
for the Kingfisher':

Prayer is like watching for the
Kingfisher. All you can do is
Be there where he is like to appear, and
Wait.
Often nothing much happens;
There is space, silence and
Expectancy.
No visible signs, only the
Knowledge that he's been there
And may come again.
Seeing or not seeing cease to matter,
You have been prepared
But when you've almost stopped
Expecting it, a flash of brightness
Gives encouragement.

You won't see a kingfisher if you're stuck indoors, of course; we have to put ourselves out there, to be in with a chance. Walking beside a river offers the best opportunity, though there's never any guarantee. Yet there is indeed that knowledge that 'he's been there, and may come again', which keeps us ever hopeful.

* * *

Along the river, we pause again to consider the Hebrew word *Hineni*, which is spoken by several characters in the Bible (such as Abraham, Moses and Isaiah), in response to God's 'call' at key moments in their lives. It means, 'Here I am!' and carries with it a sense of vulnerability, of offering one's whole self.

For us here today, it's almost like a gateway into the present moment. *Here I am!*

So in the stillness of a near perfect autumn afternoon, as sunlight angles upwards from the surface of the water to cast its warming glow on our faces, we close our eyes and imagine that God is calling our own name, over and over, as if waking us, gently, from sleep.

We then respond, inwardly: '*Hineni*: Here I am.' Present to God, to the river and trees, to the birds and the clouds; to this afternoon and its capacity for healing and reconnection.

And slowly, we open our eyes. Perhaps a little wider than before. You can, of course, perform this act of quiet dedication wherever you are inclined to. But it's hard to beat a riverside in autumn.

On growth and form

A pair of swans, their cygnets now departed, enhances the tranquillity of the scene, while opposite, a weeping willow's dense, leafy branches flow in sinuous waves from at least 40 feet (12 m) at the top of the crown to almost touch the river.

The healing qualities of extracts from willow leaves and bark have been known for several thousand years. Gerard's

Herball *(1597) describes the restorative qualities of willow for those with fevers, or with corns and 'other like risings in the feet and toes'. Research has now confirmed that willow bark contains salicin, a chemical similar to aspirin, with powerful pain-relieving and anti-inflammatory effects.*

The graceful form of this willow also reminds me of the insights of D'Arcy Thompson, the Scottish scientist and mathematician, in his ground-breaking book On Growth and Form. *It was first published in 1917 but has been revised and reprinted many times and is described as the finest work of literature in the annals of science.*

Thompson analyses the growth and form of a wide variety of living organisms from a mathematical perspective, such as the structure of plankton, the spiral of a snail's shell and the distribution of the leaves along the stem of a flowering plant.

He concludes that the perfection of mathematical beauty is such that 'whatsoever is most beautiful and regular [in the living world] is also found to be most useful and excellent'. It is an eloquent expression of the order that is inherent in the growth, form and functioning of all life, including the willow tree, and us.

* * *

Our walk now takes us through the water meadows, on a narrow path that follows a lively tributary. A kestrel launches itself not far above us, and hovers with grace, head completely still, its attention fixed with absolute focus on the ground below. Imagine if we could bring such attention to whatever or whoever is before us.

There's a glorious tangle of ripeness and decay, all around: berries, seeds, a myriad fallen leaves mouldering away. Broken stalks stand brittle and half-snapped, grasses withering, brambles knotting, all destined for descent into mulch.

Sometimes we have to let things fall. And that's not necessarily just the big dramatic stuff of life and death, but the ordinary in-between things that will come, and must, in time, go: the happy holidays that draw to an end; the project we've enjoyed working on, which we now have to hand over; the dear friend who is moving away from the area ...

There is a certain spiritual comfort to be drawn from watching a leaf fall to the ground, and surrendering yourself, and knowing that it's part of the mystery, part of the *yield*.

We matter. And we will un-matter, too.

* * *

I love the story of the acorns, as told by Cynthia Bourgeault in her book *The Wisdom Way of Knowing*. Once upon a time, a brown and capless acorn is dropped by a bird into a group of proud, shiny green acorns nestling by the trunk of a great oak tree. These beautiful specimens, who spend all their time and effort on their outward appearance (and religiously attending self-help courses such as 'Getting All You Can Out of Your Shell'), are offended by the newcomer's presence, and by the ludicrous tale he starts to tell. Looking up to the oak tree, he stammers out, 'We ... are ... *that*.' Of course we're not, think the other acorns, but one of them indulges him anyway, and asks how on Earth they might become like that tree. It has something to do with going into the ground, he replies, and cracking open the shell.

'Insane,' they responded. 'Totally *morbid*. Why, then we wouldn't be acorns anymore.'

The wanderings of water

Since medieval times, the fields of the Itchen Valley south of Winchester have been grazed with livestock and maintained as water meadows, a characteristic feature of many English river valleys. To create water meadows, the main river is divided into several side-streams, which have been dug by human hand, and the flow of water through them controlled by opening or closing sluices and drains. This keeps the surrounding fields moist, particularly through the spring and summer, and brings more nutrients to the grass to enrich its growth. As a result, there is better pasture for livestock and the prospect of larger crops of hay.

During the first half of the twentieth century the practice declined, as artificial fertilizers were developed and labour became too costly. These changes had a damaging impact on wildlife; water vole and dragonfly numbers dropped dramatically, for example, as many of the streams were filled in to create more land. However, it's encouraging to see that some areas of these Itchen water meadows, previously overgrown, are being cleared by the Hampshire Wildlife Trust, and willow saplings planted alongside old tree stumps.

Brian encourages us to find somewhere to pause, along the path, to take a few deeper breaths and to relax into our surroundings. As a Sanskrit proverb puts it, 'Breath is life, and if you breathe well you will live long on Earth.' Research confirms the benefits of the regular practice of deep breathing, such as reduced anxiety and feelings of stress; lower blood pressure; increased energy levels and relaxed muscles.

It is also good for us simply to gaze at the sky, the clouds, the trees, the grass, and to give thanks to the God of creation for the sheer wonder of our existence: for the fact that if the Earth was fractionally nearer or further away from the sun, life as we know it would be impossible; for the vital, life-giving substance that is water; for the amazing balance of the interactions between plants, animals and the gases of the atmosphere that provide us with oxygen and remove exhaled carbon dioxide ...

It is all, in a sense, a miracle.

Facing uphill

St Catherine's Hill begins to rise magnificently into view, a little way to the east of the water meadows, and a full 106 yards (97 m) above them, and that's where we're headed.

We're going to take the steep way up, and it will challenge our fitness. But this is our chance to offer a prayer that speaks louder than words about our suffering. Sometimes we just can't fathom why bad things happen to good people; why a friend has fallen ill, or why we've lost our job so suddenly. It needn't be extreme suffering, either; many of us simply struggle, in a low-grade, unspectacular way, just to stay mentally well in today's fast-paced culture.

Bringing our perplexity, as a form of walking prayer through our body, as we struggle up the hill, is a poignant and cathartic act. After all, our suffering can bring us closer to God, so long as we bring our suffering *to* God.

A close friend of mine has just been diagnosed with cancer, and my prayer is for her, as I lean into the hill, and the hill tests me.

* * *

St Catherine's offers commanding views over Winchester and the surrounding countryside. The hilltop is encircled by the ridge and ditch of a circular Iron Age hill fort. At the centre, a clump of beech trees covers the foundations of St Catherine's Chapel, built about 900 years ago and destroyed in 1537. St Catherine is known as the patron saint of hilltops – many are named after her – and perhaps the circular shape of the fort prompted a memory that she was martyred on a wheel.

On the way up, red admirals are basking in the late autumn sunshine, before finding a sheltered space for the winter. A gentle humming sound ahead of us is coming from an extensive growth of ivy, winding its way up an old hawthorn. Ivy's 'late flowering' provides a welcome source of nectar for insects, and this particular ivy is covered with bees, wasps and flies enjoying the feast, and reminding us of Keats' poetic imagery.

Approaching the top of the hill, we crunch through piles of bronze, wind-blown beech leaves, waiting for some rain to trigger the process of decay. There's a profound sense that the natural world is having one last gasp of activity before hunkering down for the winter and its essential processes of death and decomposition, to be followed by re-birth next spring.

* * *

It's a relief to reach the summit. Nothing lasts for ever, even though it often feels that the difficult times will.

Roots from a line of great beech trees are exposed from the banks of the ancient fortifications. Someone has hung a rope swing from a branch, a huge long branch that resembles a giant's arm, and Rachel, a writer, feels the urge to be playful. She grabs the makeshift handle, a snapped-off branch, lifts her knees and like a child she flies through the air, as the rest of us vicariously savour the thrill.

A few metres further along the ancient ditch and we're out into the open. The place itself has a mysterious air, and little seems to have changed up here since Keats walked this way, observing that 'the air is worth sixpence a pint'. (Although there is the M3, of course, which so infamously cut Twyford Down in two, and separated this hill – and its fragile ecosystem – from the rest of the downlands. There is now talk of a 'green bridge' to let the wildlife join back up.)

There before us is a maze of grooves cut a few inches deep into the plateau, square in shape and about ten by ten metres. This is known as the 'mis-maze' – though it's a single path, just like the labyrinth in Romsey – and we're here to walk it, to press in symbolically and prayerfully towards the heart of the afternoon, the season, and our own place within it.

It's believed to have been dug in the seventeenth century, possibly by a Winchester College boy, but no one knows for sure. What we do know is that it's an atmospheric place to practise a walking meditation. We'll use some words from Psalm 16 today, 'Make known to me the path of life', as we go, and speak them inwardly, like a mantra. You don't have to, of course. You could simply notice what you notice as you walk, or synchronize your footsteps with your breathing as a form of meditation, or bring a question 'in' with you as you walk towards the centre.

The path is narrow; it's more of a groove. But it's filled with the golden-brown beech leaves, and it's as if, today, we are following a golden thread towards the middle.

We hold a powerful silence together once we arrive at the centre, as the wind guides a few more leaves into our huddled midst, and we stand within the air, within the sky, and within the dwindling light.

Hineni: here *we* are.

And who knows whether, around this day 3,000 years or so ago, a group of Celts didn't gather too, close to this very spot, to light fires and to prepare themselves for the darker winter days to come.

Thou hast thy music too

The closing stage of today's journey takes us down a long flight of steps on the south side of St Catherine's Hill where late-flowering harebells take fragile shelter in the hollows made by the steps themselves.

Distant views of harvested fields along the Itchen Valley remind us sadly that Keats' reaper in his poem 'To Autumn', whose 'hook spares the next swath and all its twined flowers', would no longer see an abundance of wild flowers among the corn. Chemical sprays have sterilized the fields so that the crop grows undisturbed by 'weeds'. Thankfully, farmers are now encouraged to set aside areas around the edges and headlands of their fields so that wild flowers such as poppies, cornflowers and scarlet pimpernel can begin to flourish once more.

* * *

We descend, conscious of carrying something of the connection we've just made with us, something of the goodness of this saunter back, as gift, to the people and places from which we have come, today, and to which we are returning.

It is a challenge, when life is busy and often fraught. One of our group shares with me that she has recently returned from humanitarian work in a war-torn country. She has connected with a peace today that will help to settle her soul, and to breathe life into her future work. Retreating, after all, is not about merely recovering from the work we've done, but about creating a prayerful space out of which our action flows; action that is poised, creative, compassionate, courageous, filled with life and energy and love.

In the meantime, we've also tuned back in to the slow, steady work of autumn upon *us*. To the yielding *and* the yield.

It's getting dark as we retrace our steps along a narrow path by the river's edge. I happen to be out in front, walking with Esther, when all at once, breathtakingly, a kingfisher arrows up the river beside us. Not only that, but it comes to rest in an oak tree overhanging the water – and we are all able to gather, in silent wonder, to watch. To let awe turn to wonder, which turns to gratitude, which turns to prayer.

Esther is more than jubilant; she's positively overflowing. The Holy Spirit once appeared as a dove, but it feels as if she's back, tonight, and robed in kingfisher blue.

* * *

We arrive back at the cathedral just in time for evensong. Milli, an artist, shares with us that today has been 'a window of joy and hope'. The combined choir of men's and boys' voices creates a sublime, other-worldly atmosphere for worship, and the words of Keats' ode seem to rise with them: 'Where are the songs of spring? Ay, Where are they? Think not of them, thou hast thy music too.'

Our walk today has reminded us, in so many ways, that autumn does indeed have its music, literal and metaphorical. Though we so often fear this season's arrival, there is a divine mystery about it, and today we have heard its song afresh.

Activities

- Go out for a walk, and simply watch for something in nature that catches your attention. Instead of walking past, stop – and allow yourself to stay rooted, for several minutes, contemplating it. Just watch it closely.

- Find an indoor space that really inspires you, and imagine that you carry something of its beauty or peace within you. Try also to nurture that sense of space 'around' you, through your presence.
- Remind yourself of your favourite book, poem or artwork, and revisit it. How might it have helped to inspire you?
- Taking the word *Hineni*, stand outside in a favourite spot (or just in your garden) and imagine God calling your name, over and over, for a couple of minutes at least. When you are ready, then respond (quietly out loud, if you have privacy, otherwise inwardly) by saying, '*Hineni*, here I am.' Consciously 'present' yourself, to the moment, to the place, to God.
- Arrange a contemplative walk with a small group, perhaps on an old pilgrimage route or between some ancient churches in the countryside – and add a few questions for contemplation.
- Keep watch for a kingfisher. And wait and watch for a glimpse of the divine presence as you do so, in prayer.

11

November
To Deepen the Love

A walk in the footsteps of Arthur Tansley,
pioneer of nature reserves, at Kingley Vale,
among its ancient yews

You may walk freely among the dark religious trees, with
trunks like huge, rudely fashioned pillars of red and purple
iron-stone. One has the sensation of being in a vast cathedral;
not like that of Chichester, but older and infinitely vaster;
fuller of light and gloom and mystery, and more wonderful
in its associations.
(W. H. Hudson, nineteenth-century naturalist and writer)

* * *

Kingley Vale National Nature Reserve, although hidden away
in a fold of the South Downs a few miles from Chichester,

West Sussex, has one of the finest yew forests in Europe, with many very ancient trees. It's also the resting place of Sir Arthur Tansley, a founding father of the science of ecology, and an early champion of Britain's nature 'reserves'.

So Brian and I, with our love of old trees and our desire to find new places to explore, couldn't resist making this the focus for November's walk.

There are few signposts to the reserve – it's a hidden gem – but we are able to find a small car park just west of the village of West Stoke. A gravel track takes walkers a mile or so to the entrance, passing through wooded farmland that provides few clues of the delights to come.

* * *

It's the kind of weather you normally retreat *from*, not into. Grey, formless clouds above, and fallen leaves below, rotting into the mud beneath our already dew-soaked boots. This hinterland between autumn and winter can seem like a strange, almost featureless blur. As Thomas Hood wrote in his 1844 poem 'November',

> No sun – no moon!
> No morn – no noon!
> No dawn – no dusk – no proper time of day …
> November!

At least with the cold, crisp days of a deep mid-winter, you know where you stand. Nevertheless, Howard and I remind ourselves that here, within the greyness of November, this *is* where we stand; and, as we have learned from our walks so far, every time and every place issues a unique invitation of its own. The challenge is to receive it.

And for me, the invitation arrives almost the moment we step out of the car and begin to breathe the fresh Sussex air: *slow your beating heart, quieten your chattering mind, tune in to a different frequency.*

I've been a little overwhelmed recently, a feeling that has intensified today, having lost an hour or two this morning to the kind of computer problems – forgotten passwords and infuriating log-in issues – that just make you want to give up. It feels toxic in a way you can't put your finger on. I'm aware, standing within this fresh air, that it's not time-management skills and IT competency I need most pressingly, but some kind of touch. A healing touch, perhaps. I yearn to be back in touch again, with nature, with God, with who I really am.

Into the yews

The grey and damp November day is brightened by the colours of late flowers and a few autumn trees still with their leaves: the yellow of autumn hawkbit and the blue of scabious; shades from white to deep mauve of yarrow; the gold and bronze of the oaks and beeches.

We're walking along a gently sloping valley with dense wood-land on either side. The grey, gaunt skeletons of the majority of leafless trees provide an eerie contrast to the dark green, almost black, of the old yew trees that tower above the main canopy.

The yew has a long and sometimes dark history that is steeped in myth and folklore. Was it the tree on which the warrior god Odin hanged himself? Did English yew wood provide staves for the longbows that secured victory at the Battle of Agincourt in 1415?

For the Druids of Celtic Britain, the evergreen was symbolic of the regenerative power of nature and the 'most perfect symbol for everlasting life' (according to Fred Hageneder, a member of the Ancient Yew Group). With Christianity, yew came to symbolize the resurrection (yew shoots would be buried with the dead), and played a part in Easter celebrations (its branches would be used as 'palms'). Although yews are typically found in churchyards, it's thought that many predate the churches – which were built upon what were already considered to be sacred sites.

In his fascinating book The Englishman's Flora, *Geoffrey*

Grigson writes: 'Various properties combined to suggest power and peculiarity in yew trees: they live to a great age, the timber is hard ("a post of yew outlives a post of iron"), the leaves are poisonous, and the berries are red.'

But for Brian and me it is probably their amazing longevity, in particular, that has drawn us to Kingley Vale. Some of the trees here are thought to be more than a thousand years old. The best of them are on the right-hand side of the valley along a way-marked nature trail; about 20 gnarled and twisting 'ancients'.

* * *

The sign takes us off the main path and into the grove.

It's as if you can feel the trees' presence before you see them. Is that my imagination, I wonder, or something more real than real? I can believe that there is something in the air here; after all, 'here' is where these great forms have gathered themselves over so much time that time seems irrelevant. We laugh as we glimpse our first ancient yew. Why? I wonder. Why does joy seem to rise, no matter how we might be feeling, as we step into nature?

We keep going, deeper into the grove, to find ourselves increasingly among Hudson's 'dark, religious trees'. Dark is the right word, too; the trees *are* dark, and the air thick; after all, the sickly November light can barely penetrate this ever-green canopy above. Hudson is right on another thing, too – it *is* like walking into a cathedral, but better, and we find ourselves now whispering reverentially in hushed tones.

Here now before us is one great, vast tree, several metres in girth, sinewy, coiled, monstrous almost. Gloriously alive, in a state of suspended animation. As the poet Wordsworth wrote in his poem 'Lorton Vale':

Huge trunks! and each particular trunk a growth
Of intertwisted fibres serpentine
Up-coiling.

And this tree here has done something monumental over the centuries. Its brute branches first rise, but then stretch outwards and plunge downwards to the forest floor, some going right *into* the ground, and rising up again like new trees, to form a natural ring, many metres in circumference, on the bare reddish earth around the tree. Brambles guard the outer perimeter as if they know there is something special to protect about the space within.

* * *

Crawling into this space – and it does require crawling – reminds me of the days I'd crawl, as a little boy, under the over-sized tablecloth at home when the table was laid, to hide. And this is a magnificent hiding place. There aren't many places left to hide in today's culture, especially when our phones are constantly on.

Here is where we choose to take twenty minutes of complete stillness, in the tree's presence. Howard goes round to the other side of the circle, while I rest on a great branch that has fallen. It is so expansive that I can lie comfortably upon it and close my eyes.

As I begin to tune in, I imagine *it* tuning in to me, too.

After a while, I move to the trunk, dig my feet into the ground and lean against it. It's as if it holds me; and I feel *borne*, along with the weight I have been carrying, the weight of the world, in a sense.

I feel as if I could cry.

Again, I close my eyes. Smoothness against my back. We are in touch. I wonder, is the tree pleased to feel my own close presence? It would be entirely wrong to anthropomorphize this ancient being, yet it does *seem* to offer a welcome.

Finally I sense a strength – the magnificent strength of the tree, yes – but it's as if there's a strength that resides in me, somehow, too. A God-given strength, which feels in nature very different from the fear-driven 'strength' that we usually try to summon in times of attack or threat. No, here is strength that comes through the assuredness of being; a gentleness, in fact – which seems like a contradiction in terms. This, I guess, is the very strength of love itself.

* * *

We had set a gentle alarm, so as not to worry about time keeping, but it rings way too soon. What's twenty minutes compared with a thousand years? I wanted this to go on and on; I think we both could have stayed all day.

'And in the dusk of thee, the clock/ Beats out the little lives of men,' wrote Tennyson in his poem 'In Memoriam A. H. H.', about walking in this particular grove of yews. Addressing one, he acknowledges that, in gazing upon it, he grows 'incorporate into thee'. Perhaps we were 'incorporate' all along, but it takes pausing like this to remember most truly the nature, the soulful nature, of our deepest relationships.

Howard's face is relaxed, as he emerges, with flask in hand. He, too, has sensed a strength, a peace. He has experienced his own form of communion.

I really don't know what has happened to me personally in that grove, but something has. And as we crawl out from beneath the skirts of this great sheltering tree and continue onwards, I'm – what is it? Washed clean? Reset? It isn't magic. But it feels like a healing, and its effects will last way beyond the day.

* * *

The psychotherapist Gerald May writes in his powerful book *The Wisdom of Wilderness* how he discovered healing within nature. Even as a professional he was unable to put into words quite what happened; he simply felt healed. 'We have been fractured … broken off from the nature of our world, broken away from the nature of one another, broken apart from our own nature', he writes.

> We must allow ourselves to be healed. And we must allow the rest of Nature to help us. I do not know how the healing

happens; I only know a little bit of what has happened to me. I am sure you have had some experience of it.

It can happen in ordinary situations, like feeling your hands in the dirt of a garden or lying on your back in a field. In part, it happens just through the physical touch of earth and sky and growing things. This physical healing touch has to go deep within us to where we are truly broken. For me, the deep touching happens when my mind stops and my senses open and I am given willingness. But it has to come through grace ...

For most of us, it won't be a dramatic one-off solution, but something we have to be intentional about returning to, daily or weekly. A practice to cultivate. Get outside. Find a tree, or a river, or watch the clouds from your window if that's all you can do. But let nature touch you.

As Howard points out to me, a common theme running through several of the well-known nature books he's read recently is the potential for healing from time spent engaging with living things and the natural world – such as Richard Mabey's *Nature Cure* (2005), Helen Macdonald's *H is for Hawk* (2014) and Amy Liptrot's *The Outrun* (2016).

Drop thy still dews

We emerge from this sheltered woodland space into the open downland expanse of Kingley Vale, and as we cross the valley to the edge of the 'young yew forest' – a dense stand of trees with nothing growing beneath them and thought to be a mere hundred years old – we pass a dew pond.

Dew ponds, also known as cloud ponds or mist ponds, are an important feature of the South Downs, providing sources of water for grazing animals in an environment that lacks natural streams and ponds. They are man-made, typically round and shallow with a clay or chalk lining to reduce water loss by drainage. Despite the name, dew ponds are usually replenished by rain water rather than dew or mist.

They date back to Anglo-Saxon times and possibly much

earlier. The Kingley Vale pond is unusual as it is in the valley bottom rather than on a hilltop. However, a location lower down in the valley has an advantage in reducing water loss from the pond by evaporation.

Dew ponds provide an important habitat for aquatic insects and their larvae. As we pause by the pond, we become aware of small midge-like insects dancing around our heads, and we start instinctively swiping the air to avoid being bitten. In fact, they are probably winter gnats performing their courtship dances, which, unlike the summer midges, don't bite!

Swarms of winter gnats are sometimes called 'hauntings', a delightful collective noun that well describes the ghostly hovering of these insects as they buzz in and out of view in the dull November light.

* * *

How comforting, the thought of a dew pond collecting refreshment in an otherwise 'dry' landscape, such as this valley. It makes us wonder how we might create our own dew ponds in the often dry valleys of our day-to-day life. Intentional ways to collect refreshment within the busyness; humble watering holes to draw from.

Giving thanks is one form of 'dew pond', of course. Counting blessings, gathering them up, letting gratitude overflow.

Pausing for breath is another. We stand still, beside this still little pond, and let the deeper stillness of the landscape settle into us. Here is a sense of togetherness, of nature at peace with itself, as a whole.

And the words of John Greenleaf Whittier, and the tune of his sublime hymn 'Dear Lord and Father of Mankind', can't help but trickle into our consciousness:

Drop thy still dews of quietness
Till all our strivings cease.
Take from our souls the strain and stress
And let our ordered lives confess
The beauty of thy peace.

There is nothing quite like sensing peace within a place, and allowing it to help you find peace with yourself. It's possibly the greatest gift of all.

* * *

Another helpful way to collect dew is through the words of Psalm 46: 'Be still and know that I am God.' I like to repeat them quietly, before entering stillness. And if it feels too much pressure to 'know', then why not try to be curious about God, instead? The writer Elizabeth Gilbert explains in her book on creativity, *Big Magic*, that curiosity provides a kindly and creative alternative to certainty. 'It is so accessible and available, every single day of my life,' she writes. 'Give attention to your curiosity.'

She goes on to suggest: 'Be still, and … *wonder*: at what you don't yet know about God's place within this place; *listen*: for what peace sounds like, within nature; *imagine*: what God loves about this particular moment; *watch*: for where your curiosity takes you …' Be still, and be curious.

The finest view in England

We're almost in a natural bowl, here – it's like an amphitheatre. There are tree-covered slopes to our left and right, and a steep grass incline in front of us, rising 200 metres to the top of the vale.

A climb always seems worth it once you've reached the top, and at our summit we encounter a herd of friendly cattle which Howard identifies as Belted Galloways – named thanks to the broad white vertical 'belt' across their otherwise black and shaggy coats. They look entirely huggable, in fact.

The cattle are grazing around the slopes of two distinct hillocks. Howard informs me, his map flapping rebelliously in the breeze, that these mounds are known as the Devil's Humps. They are Bronze Age 'round barrows', shaped perfectly for cycling up and over, which is probably why there's a sign forbidding it. Nearby, he notes from the map, are remains of a Romano-Celtic temple, an Iron Age settlement and pre-historic flint mines – all signs of the human habitation that predates the yew trees down below.

We encounter more wildlife – this time, in the form of two teenagers and their parents, who are out on a walk and marvel-ling at the cattle, as well as the sheep which look like they've had a blow-dry, their grey wool frizzing into a coiffure. We talk together about the sloeberries on the bushes, the animals, and just how good it is to be outside.

For a moment, we all stand there together in a not-*too*-awkward silence, strangers, admiring the view, which *is* special: stretching as far as the eye can see, out to Chichester harbour and beyond, the fields in the foreground obligingly making a patchwork quilt of English countryside, and the dew pond now a mere droplet below.

We aren't the first to tap into its magic. As well as those ancient settlers who buried their dead up here on the hill, the future King Charles II is reputed to have stopped here, while fleeing from defeat at the Battle of Worcester in 1651, and, looking down upon its beauty, exclaimed, 'England is surely worth fighting for.'

Two and a half centuries later, Arthur Tansley, who we've come in part to pay homage to, was to feel similarly, as he beheld this same vista and described it as 'the finest in England'. He, like Charles, could see that it was worth fighting for, but this time the battle was for nature's preservation itself.

Sir Arthur Tansley

We've climbed the hill not just to admire the view but to go in search of a memorial stone to Tansley, who was an English botanist, a pioneer of the science of ecology, and crucially one of the founders of nature conservation in Britain.

Until the beginning of the twentieth century, professional biologists had focused their research primarily on the classifica-tion, anatomy and physiology of individual plants and animals.

Scientists such as Tansley began to broaden their interests, however, observing and describing associations of plants and animals in their natural habitats.

As a result of these developments in biology, words such as 'ecology' (the relationships of living things to each other and their environment) and 'ecosystem' (a system of interacting organisms and their environment) are now in common use. It was Tansley who first promoted the wider use of the word 'ecosystem', and he could see that an understanding of the relationships between living organisms and their environment was fundamental for the conservation of nature.

His conclusions point directly to the inter-connectedness of all life on Earth, and of inanimate matter. Everything joins up, and there are consequences – often dire – if we lose any single part of the whole complex jigsaw of life or if we break the links between the parts.

* * *

Sometimes it might feel awkward for people like Howard and me, as Christians, to think of the world as a 'whole' – as a living, breathing being. Isn't that all a bit New Age, a bit pagan? But this is surely where the science helps to point us, as well as the 'earthed' form of Celtic Christian spirituality which writers such as John Philip Newell espouse.

Newell writes, drawing upon Celtic theology: 'The matter of Creation is a holy and living energy born from the hidden depths of God. The universe is a single organism that carries within itself one ancient rhythm. It is a body with one heartbeat.'

That shouldn't diminish our sense of uniqueness within it all, nor of God's sustaining presence coursing through it; but it helps me to realize that, instead of simply being individual actors upon the neutral stage of the universe, we are very much part of the same living body. Everything we do affects everything else. Our actions have consequences. The smallest of lifestyle choices have knock-on effects, which is heartening news for those of us who feel we can't make a difference in the world.

As Thomas Berry writes in his book *The Sacred Universe*:

> The deepest mystery of all ... is surely the manner in which ... [all] forms of life, from the plankton in the sea and the bacteria in the soil to the giant sequoia or to the most massive mammals, are ultimately related to one another in the comprehensive bonding of all the life systems. Genetically speaking, every living being is coded not only in regard to its own interior processes, but in relation to the entire complex of earthly being. This is to be alive and to be the fertile source of life.

As he reiterates so deftly elsewhere in *Evening Thoughts*, 'We are a communion of subjects, not a collection of objects.'

* * *

In 1904, Tansley proposed the formation of a central organization for the systematic survey and mapping of the vegetation of the British Isles. This became the British Vegetation Committee, which in 1913 spawned the British Ecological Society. The most significant part of Tansley's work was eventually published in 1939 as a comprehensive study, The British Islands and their Vegetation.

During World War Two, as thoughts began to turn to the reconstruction of post-war Britain, Tansley chaired a committee of the British Ecological Society that formulated a policy on nature reserves and led to the founding of The Nature Conservancy in 1949. Kingley Vale was one of the very first National Nature Reserves to be established in Britain in 1952, and so this area was protected in perpetuity. Tansley died in 1955 and, at his request, his ashes were scattered here in Kingley Vale.

Although not a household name, Tansley was a crucial founding father of nature conservation in Britain. The County Wildlife Trusts and national conservation organizations such as the RSPB are a powerful legacy for a great scientist who was passionate about understanding and protecting the natural world. Raising money and seeking volunteers for conservation projects is easier if the wildlife at risk is big, beautiful or cuddly but, for the long-term survival of Planet Earth as a healthy place to live, we should be as concerned about every species of moss or fly that is threatened with extinction. They all play their vital parts in the great web of life, as Tansley, who was knighted for his services to conservation, demonstrated.

After following several false trails, we discover his memorial stone, sheltered by a small clump of trees but with spectacular views south towards the coast and the inlets of Chichester harbour, looking out upon the view he loved most.

* * *

The stone is a simple and humble monument, tucked back almost within the trees at the top of the hill. What's inscribed there is well worth finding. A simple epitaph to a truly great man:

> He strove with success ...
> to widen the knowledge,
> deepen the love,
> and safeguard the heritage
> of nature
> in the British Isles.

What a way to sum up a life!

Thanks to this man, we are able to understand better the relationship we have to the natural world, of which we are a part, and thus to deepen our love.

And his epitaph is a wonderful reminder to ask ourselves, too: What are we striving for? How will we know when we are successful? What kind of love do we hope to deepen? And how would we like to be remembered?

* * *

The stone's inscription inspires us to reflect on the nature of our lives, and brings to mind John O'Donohue's suggestion, in his book Eternal Echoes, *that we should take the time to 'make' a prayer that will become the prayer of our soul:*

> *Listen to the voices of longing in your soul. Listen to your hungers. Give attention to the unexpected that lives around the rim of your life. Listen to your memory and the onrush of your future, to the voices of those near you and those you have lost. Out of all that ... make a prayer ... that is worthy of the destiny to which you have been called.*

It's a bit like an epitaph in advance, and it's worth doing. For although few of us will achieve the worldly recognition of a person such as Sir Arthur Tansley, we shall all leave a legacy – most importantly, and apart from our work, among our family and friends. Really, our life is the prayer of our soul – but it's a valuable exercise to try to put something in writing, to express the nature of the 'prayer of your soul' in words. It might take a month or a year, but it will provide an opportunity to recognize the call within you and to reflect on the qualities you would like to see within your own legacy.

The most ancient rhythm of love

We're touched, too, that Tansley's inscription speaks not just of a widening knowledge but also of a deepening *love*. For love is such an important word when it comes to our relationships, after all, including (crucially) our relationship with nature.

It is also an ever-deepening word; for the more we love, the deeper we can go.

When it comes to nature, we probably start with quite a superficial sense of love. 'I love nature,' we might say. But it's usually a self-centred form of love, more about me than it is about creation. 'I love being out here, because it does me good.'

Yet love, of course, implies an active, two-way flow. A healthy love is not about dependency, but a mutual flourishing, care, respect, inter-connectedness.

And certainly on a day like today, even within the gloom of this November grey-scape, it's possible to find yourself deeper within an ecosystem that isn't just physical, but emotional, mental, spiritual. The ecosystem of love, we might call it, of which we are all invited to find our own unique identity, and to play our own humble, inter-dependent part.

When John Philip Newell writes of the universe being a single living being with a single heartbeat, he fleshes it out to this very end: that the universe carries within it 'one ancient rhythm: love'. 'That is the beat at the heart of all things,' he affirms. 'The first and deepest sound within the unfolding cosmos.'

So when we find ourselves loving, and being loved, perhaps that's when we are most fully in touch with this living, breathing universe. God's life is God's love, and we have the privilege of embodying a conscious expression of such love within the world.

You only have to pause, for a short while, to feel your own heart beating, and to give thanks for the gift of life and love, to find yourself back in touch with that pulsing rhythm.

All of which helps to deepen the love that Howard and I share for our Creator, too, who we sense is indeed very much here, within us, between us, and beyond us: in the energy of the wind, in the wisdom of the ages, in the magnificence of the buzzard overhead, in the endurance and healing of a tree, in the decomposition of muddied leaves, in the peace of the dew pond, and the vastness of the horizon.

The fruits of the land

Negotiating the steep slope back down the hill, we have to keep our eyes on the muddy track beneath our feet to avoid a much more rapid descent into the valley than we had planned. But we become aware of two features of the landscape around us, in particular. First, the sound of silence as the deepening mist darkens the November dusk, broken only by the occasional and eerily raucous cry of a jay, pheasant or crow.

We can't help noticing, too, the extensive and striking

growths of old man's beard, the wild version of garden clematis, covering the shrubs at the woodland edge with its flowing grey 'beards' of long feathery seeds.

Wild clematis has a delightful variety of local names including traveller's joy, grandfather's whiskers, devil's guts, hedge feathers and skipping ropes. Geoffrey Grigson explains that several of the names derive from the fact that the stems were smoked by local people: 'It is Boy's Bacca because boys (as well as gipsies – gipsy's bacca – and shepherds – shepherd's delight – and the poor generally – poor man's friend) smoked cigar lengths of the dried stems, which draw well and do not burst into flame.'

A wander through Kingley Vale two or three hundred years ago would surely have produced most of the foods, medicines, pleasures and other daily needs of the locals for free.

Towards the bottom of the slope, a small but old wayfaring-tree stands as a solitary sentinel among the dead grasses and herbs. Its leaves and berries would once have been used for gargling and settling the stomach, and for making black hair dye. It is a characteristic shrub of the chalk downs in the south of England, bearing blue-green leaves with distinctive white undersides and large clusters of white flowers throughout the spring and early summer. At this time of year, just a few black fruits remain.

It is almost dark as we return to where we started, at the yew grove, and Brian is stopped in his tracks by several bright green patches of moss that cover a sprawling elder tree. They seem to be glowing with a cold light of phosphorescence in the gloom of an autumn evening. This magical moment wonderfully confirms our rich range of experiences during the walk through Kingley Vale.

We make a final short diversion from the footpath back into the woodland to say goodbye, and thank you, to the ancient yews. A nearby interpretive board seems to sum up our feelings rather beautifully. It reads:

For centuries these yew trees have been one of the few constant features in the landscape. Legend and myth cling to them *like autumn mist. The haunt of pagan druids, a memorial to the victorious Saxon warriors of Chichester, stalked by the ghost of the poet Tennyson, clinging to the thin chalk soils. They will outlive us all.*

Indeed they will. And in the meantime, we agree, as we head back to the car park, they will live lovingly within our hearts, too, for as long as those hearts continue to beat.

Activities

- Find a 'secret place' you can visit outside, somewhere you can go to get away from it all, and visit it regularly to rest and dwell.
- Consider a 'dew pond' you could create in your schedule, perhaps by pausing regularly to breathe more deeply, to walk more slowly, to give thanks, or – by turning off your electronic devices habitually – to refresh yourself and regain a balance in your everyday life.
- Visit Kingley Vale NNR to find the ancient yew grove and Tansley's memorial stone; or find another location that is high up in the countryside and is likely to have prehistory associated with it (Bronze and Iron Age and/or Romano-Celtic sites). Spend time absorbing the long history of the place, the beauty of the surroundings.
- 'Be still, and ...' be curious!
- Draft your own simple epitaph. How would you love to be remembered?
- Try writing the 'prayer of your soul'. You don't need to finish it straight away. 'Give attention ...' to the unexpected that lives around the rim of your life.

12

December
The Winter Wander on the Solstice

A walking retreat at Stockbridge Down, Hampshire

It is 2pm on 21 December, as we gather, with a group of hardy folk, for a saunter on Stockbridge Down in Hampshire. It is also quite a contrast to when Brian and I were here last, six months to the day, to watch the sun set on the summer solstice. Today, there are only 7 hours 20 minutes of daylight, and we're here to catch the last moments of them on this, the shortest day of the year.

It's overcast and the wind-chill forces us to pull our woolly hats down hard over our ears. It's not the sort of day you might naturally choose for a walk, but as a group we've decided to face into the darkness of the gathering dusk, in a mini-retreat we've called our 'Winter Wander'.

Stockbridge Down is an area of chalk grassland and scrub easy to access from the roadside, a mile east of Stockbridge in

Hampshire. It's managed by the National Trust in conjunction with other conservation organizations and local 'commoners' who have had grazing rights on the Down since the 1300s; and its designation as a 'Site of Special Scientific Interest with Scheduled Ancient Monuments' makes this a fascinating place to visit for both its wildlife and its history.

We know from archaeological evidence that Stockbridge Down has been a place of regular human activity since at least the Bronze Age, over 4,000 years ago. Excavation of one of its thirteen tumuli (burial mounds) has revealed the skeleton of a crouched woman and a pottery beaker (drinking cup). The 'Beaker people' are known from sites across western and central Europe as a characteristic culture of late Neolithic and early Bronze Age times.

About 3,000 years ago, Iron Age inhabitants from this part of Hampshire came here to the hilltop to build a defensive fort known as Woolbury Ring. During this period, farmers were also cutting ledges (or 'lynchets') in the north-eastern slopes of the hillside to grow crops. And so, long before the Romans arrived in the area around AD 43, this had been a place for everyday life, for defence in times of tribal warfare, and for burial.

Living landscapes

So here we are, ready to enter the heart of natural darkness. It's become one of my favourite days of the year, as I've learned gradually not to be so afraid of the dark, or depressed about this time of the year, but to look for a beauty that we otherwise don't get to see in the full neon-glare of our artificially illuminated lives.

We begin, as usual, by walking slowly, as it's such a helpful way physically to leave the faster pace of life behind and to tune in, step by step, to this landscape. It's an ethereal atmosphere here, and it's not that hard to imagine men, women and children walking these downs thousands of years ago. Surely they would have paused, on this solstice day, on these very slopes, to watch the same sun setting – hoping, praying that the Earth would tilt, once more, towards the light.

We're keeping an eye on where the sun *should* be, behind us, as we set off eastwards for a walk while we still have some light. The plan is to gather back on the west-facing slopes to see the sunset in an hour or so. Stockbridge Down affords a remarkable vantage point, being one of the highest spots around, though today the sun is veiled in a curtain of thick grey cloud that seems to have no intention of opening. Never mind: being here on this day is not about creating a perfectly choreographed spiritual experience, but about being *here*, outside, in December.

The downland rises gently before us in shades of khaki greens and browns, then dips like a switchback, before lifting us to a first peak, where we can see the seemingly endless Hampshire countryside stretching before us. Or at least agricultural fields – and there's a difference ...

* * *

There is, indeed. Stockbridge Down has become an 'island' of natural habitat in a sea of intensively farmed land, leaving wildlife extremely vulnerable. The fine views remind us that we need more trees and, in particular, joined-up areas of woodland. We can see many small areas of woodland but they are surrounded by thousands of hectares of what is, for the surviving wildlife, relatively sterile farmland cultivated using the latest, toxic agrochemicals.

As consumers, we're part of this problem, but can be part of the solution too, if we're prepared to pay a little more for our food, or eat less meat, for example, so that the land can be farmed less intensively.

Conservation groups have been working hard since 2006 to join up isolated islands of natural habitat like this under the banner of an ambitious project called Living Landscapes. The Wildlife Trusts have described the challenge thus:

Nature conservation in the UK has traditionally focused on the preservation of specific sites. But outside these few places, natural habitats have been lost on an unprecedented scale and many species, both common and rare, are in long-term decline. As the demand for land for agriculture, housing and development has increased, so the room for wildlife and natural processes has decreased. This has resulted in small oases of wildlife-rich protected land, such as nature reserves, becoming surrounded by an otherwise inhospitable landscape for many plants and animals.

Living Landscapes is inspired by a vision to transform the environment we live in: restoring, recreating and reconnecting wildlife-rich spaces in rural and urban areas by working in partnership with local communities, landowners, schools and businesses. There are now over a hundred projects and although, sadly, Stockbridge Down is not on the list, places nearby such as the Itchen Valley, the Wiltshire Downs and the Isle of Wight are. Each scheme covers a large area of land, often with protected areas such as nature reserves and Sites of Special Scientific Interest (SSSIs) within them. Reserves and SSSIs are vital sanctuaries from which wildlife can re-emerge into the wider landscape once it has been restored.

* * *

The landscape right here on the Down feels eerie, bleak almost. But there's a sense of welcome, too – at least, it's a very welcome change from all the shopping and piped music as Christmas closes in. It brings relief, to look to a horizon and breathe cold, fresh air, and to smell the chalk-flecked turf. There's nothing like the whiff of soil to earth you.

Stepping outside like this intentionally can help us to integrate the rhythms of nature with the main seasonal 'event' of Christmas. Today's solstice is, of course, about light and dark – the kind of imagery that pervades the Advent story as metaphor. As the prologue to John's Gospel puts it:

What came into existence was Life,
    and the Life was Light to live by.
The Life-Light blazed out of the darkness;
    the darkness couldn't put it out.
(John 1, *The Message* version)

As we read these words together on a darkening hillside, they resonate. We're a perfectly ordinary collection of people, with an ordinarily diverse spectrum of challenges, such as illness, depression, grief, perplexity ... and we would all, I sense, love to experience something more of the life-light: not the artificial flood of 24-hour strip-lighting or false spiritual dawns – but a true light that shines from out of the very deepest darkness.

* * *

However, *first* comes the darkness, and this is always worth remembering.

We tend automatically to think of night following day, which can make us feel constantly as if the best is behind us; that evening will soon be here upon us. Spiritually, however, there's a powerful way to re-frame this. The Creation account in the book of Genesis tells us, right from the first great act of beginning, that 'There was evening, and there was morning – the first day.' And so, in this most original of understandings – which still prevails in Judaism – day follows night. Darkness is the pathway to the sun's rise. It's the womb, the start of all things new.

This brings me great heart and comfort, personally, as the nights draw in and darkness falls upon us once more.

* * *

Linked to this, Christmas doesn't fall where it does by accident. In the Early Church, Easter was the only 'historic' celebration and its date could be ascertained fairly accurately by the Jewish lunar calendar. But as the faith spread northwards, and was introduced to the Celts, much of what we now know as the 'Christian calendar' was established as the story was woven into the profound Celtic relationship to the natural world.

According to the theologian Alexander Shaia, the celebration of Jesus' birth fulfilled what the Celts had already been marking during this period of greatest darkness; this was their most important feast, because, living as they did in this cold climate, they depended on the sun's 'rebirth'.

'Nature tells the story that the Gospels amplify,' explains Shaia. And in this Advent part of the story, he says, we learn that 'the grace of the fresh radiance will come forth through our courage to walk into the deepest dark …

'The deepest dark', he says, 'is not the place where grace goes to die, but to be reborn …'

Excavating treasure

As we continue to walk, our thoughts turn to what lies under the ground, buried in the darkness. Things the eye cannot see at a casual glance. In terms of the remains of human activity, excavations on the south-western edge of Stockbridge Down have revealed the macabre evidence of a medieval execution cemetery. Among the discoveries were 40 human skeletons, two postholes – probably from gibbets – and six silver coins from the reign of Edward the Confessor.

The coins were in a small bag that had been hidden under the armpit of one of the executed malefactors and obviously missed by the gravediggers.

This ancient cemetery has been dated to about 1100 and it seems likely that the executions were punishment for breaking Forest Law. This had been introduced by the Normans, and included the death penalty for relatively minor infringements such as poaching in the king's forest.

We walk upon so many layers.

* * *

It's funny how 'place' carries with it not just traces of the distant past, but of ourselves, too. Stockbridge Down, for me, is a place where I have stored some precious memories of my own. And the end of a year is always a good time to excavate one or two; to bring up to the light some treasures that might otherwise lie hidden, and to give thanks.

Howard's mention of the buried coins takes me back to a time I'd been up here with my youngest daughter, Betsy-Joy, kicking molehills. We weren't being vandals; Howard himself had told us that moles can excavate some archaeological morsels, such as arrow heads and coins. Betsy-Joy kicked away in her green wellies with vigour, while I became distracted by the setting sun.

The next thing I knew, she was sitting on the spongy grass in tears. 'I'm never going to find a coin,' she sobbed. 'Daddy, maybe God will help me to find one, if I ask?' I confess, my heart sank: prepare for disappointment, I thought. We did ask, but seemingly to no avail.

Returning, empty-handed, I was curious to open an e-mail in which a friend mentioned finding a stash of old coins in her garage after a de-clutter. How funny, I wrote back; we'd just been searching together for coins, without joy. A day or two later, the postman delivered a parcel addressed to Betsy-Joy, and as she tore open the envelope, she discovered with great gladness ... a few of my friend's old coins. Treasure!

Two things strike me, looking back with gratitude. First, any of us can participate in the flow of God's loving kindness, if we choose to. Personally, I've little doubt God can work miracles; but I'm sure God prefers us creatively to be part of the solution for others, even if we don't always realize that we are the answer, however small, to a prayer. We might just be a gentle ray of light within someone's darkness.

Second, the real treasure, surely, is the love. It's the act itself that imbued those humble coins with their value; a precious lesson for a seven-year-old to learn (from someone she's never met), and a reminder, too, for any of us who are prone to spending our life pursuing the kind of treasure that moth and rust destroy.

* * *

Another memory burns bright, as we wander on in silence. Just last year, on New Year's Eve, I brought my children here for a walk in the dark to say goodbye to the passing year. It was one of those random, spontaneous moments. *Let's go!* Standing close to one of the Bronze Age burial mounds, we suddenly saw a bright burning light, hurtling across the sky. At first, I feared it was a crashing plane; it certainly wasn't a mere shooting star. It scored the sky from east to west for about twelve seconds, glowing green, and leaving a vivid trail of smoke. It turned out to be an exceptional meteorite (according to later reports). I'd never seen one like that, in all of my 50 years. What a gift: we ended that year, and began the next, effervescing with wonder.

What goes on in the dark, unseen

Although the track up the hillside stretches across open grassland, we can see plenty of low, turf-covered mounds, some more than a metre in diameter. Home to large colonies of yellow meadow ants, the mounds are easy to trip over if one tries to walk and admire the view at the same time! Although we see no sign of ants on the surface, much is nevertheless going on below ground. Each colony has a queen, whose only job is to lay eggs; a large number of worker ants carry out other tasks such as extending and maintaining the underground tunnels, finding food and caring for the queen.

Yellow meadow ants are rarely seen because they feed underground on the honeydew produced by root aphids, tiny insects that are relatives of greenfly. In fact, the ants are photophobic, shying away from light and preferring to live in the dark. They share this quality with a wide range of other living organisms, including filamentous fungi, the seeds of flowering plants, deep-sea fish and bats.

The ants of Stockbridge Down also have a very important role in the life cycles of the beautiful chalk-hill blue and Adonis blue butterflies, both of which are seen here in good numbers on sunny summer days. *The caterpillars of both species feed on horseshoe vetch, a low-lying plant with bright yellow flowers that is characteristic of chalk downland. Wonderfully, at the stage when the caterpillar is turning into a chrysalis, it is taken underground by the ants and protected from predators until the adult butterfly emerges. Both caterpillar and chrysalis produce a secretion that is attractive to the ants.*

This is a fascinating example of symbiosis, a relationship where two different organisms live together for their mutual benefit. Symbiosis is a challenging concept for Darwin's theory of evolution which, in its simplest and most often quoted version, is based on the idea of competition between species and the struggle for survival. We shall probably need adapted, or perhaps different, theories in the future to explain cooperative forms of behaviour that occur in the natural world. But it's worth remembering – at the most basic of levels – that life is not necessarily one endless competition, a survival of the fittest.

And today, within this group, we can appreciate the nature of giving and receiving; of mutual support, encouragement and love.

After a pause for thought, we walk on – conscious that, despite this apparently lifeless December afternoon, we are stepping over thousands of other living organisms which are going about their daily lives beneath our feet; and we resolve to return on a summer's day with a picnic, when the horseshoe vetch is flowering, amid an abundance of other small but remarkable flowering plants, and when many of the 30 or more species of butterflies that are found here will be on the wing.

Learning to see in the dark

The ants provide us with a helpful reminder that there is usually so much more to life than meets the eye. Even a bare winter tree has roots that are active, and growing, below the surface.

Spirituality is, in a sense, about learning to see differently – to be awake, alert, present – and I share with the group a powerful insight from the episcopal priest and author Barbara

Brown Taylor, from her thought-provoking book *Learning to Walk in the Dark*.

She tells the story of Jacques Lusseyran, a French resistance fighter who had gone blind at the age of eight. (As an adult he was interred in Buchenwald concentration camp, and his story is inspiring.) Ten days after losing his sight, as a boy, he made a discovery that would change the rest of his life: 'I had completely lost the sight of my eyes; I could not see the light of the world anymore,' he wrote. 'Yet the light was still there. Its source was not obliterated. I felt it gushing forth every moment and brimming over. I felt how it wanted to spread out over the world. I had only to receive it.'

Fascinatingly, he noticed that the light he saw – which wasn't just metaphorical but had a literal quality to it – changed depending upon his inner condition. The light decreased if he was fearful, sad, judgemental or competitive. Occasionally it went out altogether, and he was plunged into 'blindness'.

And here's the thing: he learned very quickly that the best way to see the inner light and remain in its presence was to *love*. As Barbara Brown Taylor concludes, 'There is a light that shines in the darkness which is only visible there.'

We close our eyes, and imagine what it is to see such light.

The meaning of awe

Our approach to the very top of the hill in the gathering gloom is made a little more challenging by a steep muddy descent into the first of the ditches that surround the south side of Woolbury Ring.

After another clamber up and down we make the final few metres of ascent to the high bank around the top of the Iron Age hill fort. There's some doubt among archaeologists and historians about the extent to which Woolbury was used as a regular and more permanent defensive position from attacking tribes; it may, in fact, have been one of an outer ring of hill forts around the main defensive position, Danebury (about four miles to the west), and used only when the local tribe was threatened.

But the view from the top is truly spectacular, offering an almost 360-degree panorama of the rolling fields of the Hampshire and Wiltshire borders. We spend a few minutes walking around the summit as the darkness of late afternoon deepens.

* * *

A final layer of memory, evoked again by *this* place, here, right at the top. A friend and I were out for a walk not long ago, up here, pondering what it means to face into the darkness of the winter – just as we're doing today – and to do it with courage and intentionality. We climbed the hill to observe night fall; and the gorgeous twilit horizons that opened up in front of us reminded me of a few lines about awe, written by the rabbi and theologian Abraham Joshua Heschel in his book *God in Search of Man*. So I pulled them up on my phone for him and began to read out loud:

> The meaning of awe is to realize that life takes place under wide horizons, horizons that range beyond the span of an individual life or even the life of a nation, a generation, or an era ... Awe enables us to perceive in the world intimations of the divine, to sense in small things the beginning of infinite significance, to sense the ultimate in the common and the simple ...

'*Look!*' my friend exclaimed, grabbing me by the shoulders.

At that precise moment, a flock of birds flew from behind us, and came so close that it seemed they flew straight through us, between us ... It was as though we were enveloped, for a few sublime moments, in a cloud of clapping wings. We stood in awed silence, not knowing what to say, and certainly not needing to say anything further. After a while, I realized I hadn't finished the Heschel passage. There was one sentence left to read, so I continued: 'To feel in the rush of the passing the stillness of the eternal.'

* * *

As we stand here now, together, as a group, we share in that sense of awe: especially 'here' within the heart of this Advent darkness, when we're also so mindful of the wonder of God being born into humanity, under these skies, and treading this Earth.

'Was there a moment, known only to God,' asks Madeleine L'Engle, the author of the classic children's novel *A Wrinkle in Time*,

> when all the stars held their breath, when the galaxies paused in their silence for a fraction of a second, and the Word, who had called it all into being, went with all his love into the womb of a young girl, and the universe started to breathe again, and the ancient harmonies resumed their song, and the angels clapped their hands for joy?

It makes me shiver to think of this (it can't just be the cold!): that the inexpressibly awesome power that formed the galaxies finds its most loving expression in the *darkness* of a human womb, and is birthed within the most common-place and simple.

Which means, I believe, that our very own humanity, too – common-place as it is – is imbued, as a result, with something like the awe of the stars. It's worth standing at the top of a hill for a few moments, just to imagine *that*. To offer yourself back, with all that you are worth. To bring everything you are to everything God is.

Trees: for shelter, pleasure and healing

Our return from Woolbury Ring, walking towards the western edge of Stockbridge Down for sunset, takes us through several small areas of scrub with a few larger trees. These help to create a more diverse range of habitats, providing food and shelter for birds, mammals and many invertebrates that would be more exposed to predators on the open grassland. We can hear the chattering of a large flock of linnets roosting in a patch of oaks, hawthorn and dogwood.

In ancient times, England had a lot more trees. It's open to debate how thick the forests had become after the climate warmed up following the Ice Age, and there is now a view that in upland areas the forests may have been more open, with substantial areas of natural grassland that were grazed by herds of wild animals such as auroch (wild cattle) and deer.

But from about 6,000 years ago, Neolithic farmers using stone tools began to clear areas of woodland, at first very slowly. They often favoured uplands, such as these downs, for their early settlements because the soils were generally lighter and easier to cultivate. It was grazing animals such as cattle, sheep, horses and goats that nibbled away the seedlings of trees and shrubs and stopped them from becoming re-established.

To bring the clock forward to the present day and Stockbridge Down, it is the cattle, sheep and horses grazing these hillsides now that keep the habitat as open, chalk grassland and prevent it from reverting to woodland. Of course, both habitats are valuable but, as we have seen on several of our walks, the chalk grassland of the downs has a unique and beautiful assemblage of flowering plants and insects, particularly orchids and butterflies.

Happily, it's home, too, to a threatened species of tree, the juniper. Juniper is a special and vulnerable tree that grows in a colony towards the eastern end of Stockbridge Down: special because it is one of only three native conifers in Britain (the others are Scots pine and yew); vulnerable because it germinates and grows slowly close to the 'mother' tree, and is easily overwhelmed by faster developing species such as dogwood and hawthorn.

In addition to the berries that are an essential flavouring for gin, juniper traditionally had a wide range of uses. Medicinally, it was seen as a 'counter-poison' and 'resister of the pestilence'. More mystically, it was a 'defence against devils, elves and witches', and was hung over doorways on the eve of May Day and burnt on Hallowe'en to ward off evil spirits. It was even used as a means to stimulate an abortion (a local name for juniper in Somerset is 'bastard killer'). The National Trust has special projects in places like the Chilterns and Stockbridge Down to nurture populations of juniper.

A chink of light, a flood of wonder

It's almost time for the moment we've been waiting for. We arrive back at the exposed west-facing side of the hill with minutes to spare before sunset, though, disappointingly, it is still behind cloud.

A red kite is poised effortlessly in flow on the currents above (how often we've been accompanied this year by a solitary bird of prey, on our walks); below, we gather in a circle. Howard has suggested that we might, within this moment, join hands. We do, and instantly there's a connection; a fragile strength, as we acknowledge – simply and without fanfare – that we do not go into the darkness alone. It feels as if it's from within the contact, the joining together as a group, that the Spirit moves and tears begin to flow, unbidden, among some of us. This is a moment of utmost connection between us, within us, and beyond us. I wonder what the red kite sees as it looks down at this transient circle of humanity. I wonder what God sees, too.

And just when it doesn't seem to matter in the slightest any more that we won't see the sunset, a chink appears in the cloud at the lowest point of the horizon, through which a decadent stream of sunlight bursts, flaring reds and yellows and golds. You couldn't make it up. The sun has waited until the very last moment to touch us with its own glory. Each face lights with a gentle radiance, and feels the benediction of warmth; this truly is a gift that remains so very hard to describe.

Thomas Berry writes movingly of the mystery of evening, and the onset of darkness:

It is a moment when some other world makes itself known, some numinous presence beyond human understanding. We experience the wonder of things as the vast realms of space overwhelm the limitations of our human minds. At this moment, as the sky turns golden and the clouds reflect the blazing colours of evening, we participate in the intimacy of all things with each other.

We do, indeed. That sense of intimacy is utterly palpable, here and now. And how interesting, that these kinds of moment are rarely diminished in the sharing (as if you somehow have to surrender a portion of the goodness to someone else); instead, they are magnified.

Who knows if this exquisite sunset is laid on just for us? It doesn't matter; we're too busy laughing and crying to worry. But through this narrowest of apertures, we know that something extraordinary and inexplicable has poured forth. As Patrick Kavanagh's poem 'Advent' puts it, 'Through a chink too wide there comes in no wonder.' Through this shortest of days, streams of wonder have poured.

We bear witness together, in the gathering darkness, to grace, reborn.

To soulful nature.

Activities

- Plan a walk, perhaps with friends, on or around the shortest day (19–23 December), to watch the sunset and to face hopefully into the natural darkness of winter.

- Use the culmination of the year to reflect on key moments from the last twelve months, things you might otherwise forget within the Christmas rush. Reflect on what these times mean for you, how they've helped to shape you, where they've taken you.

- Look for treasure in a mole hill – but use this as a reminder, too, to offer the treasure of love through small acts of kindness to those you know who struggle with the darker months of the year.

- Do some star-gazing. If you live in an area that's affected by light pollution, travel a short way to where you can better see the stars. While it's unusual to see a meteorite (a piece of space debris that has made it through the Earth's atmosphere without completely burning up), the Geminid Meteor Shower usually takes place around 13–15 December, when you can often see up to 50 shooting stars per hour, which is wonderful to watch! The Ursid Meteor Shower is sparser, but happens around the time of the solstice – so look out for that as well!

- Investigate the Wildlife Trusts' Living Landscapes projects and see if there is one accessible to you; if so, visit it and find ways to support it, if possible by volunteering with your local County Wildlife Trust.
- Search for a juniper tree. And in so doing, why not learn to identify the UK's three evergreens?
- Find a time and quiet place to read the prologue to John's Gospel (preferably outside, on a hillside, at sunrise or sunset). Let its words sink in. Read the words slowly, prayerfully.
- Plan to make a return visit around the longest day (19–23 June) to the place that you've visited on the shortest day and use some of June's activities.
- Don't be afraid to join hands, once in a while. Or give someone a hug. Make contact. The Spirit moves.

Epilogue

One of so many fond memories from this year's journey, we've decided, is sitting in the occasional pub, resting with a pint, at the end of our walks in the countryside. The soul feels at some kind of wearied and wonderful peace. There's the ache of the legs after a long day's walking. A smile shared in stillness. The satisfying quench of a thirst. The chink of a glass.

So that's where you find us, now. Cheers!

Looking back, we've walked so many miles together, and feel as if we've come quite a way. Our boots have fallen in step; souls have, too.

And the wonderful thing is, there's always more to discover, about soulful nature *and* the nature of our own soul. Just when you think you've worked it all out, you're invited deeper into the friendship of it all.

That's truly the nature of our Creator for you.

We're minded of the seasons, with whose rhythms and cycles we're a little more fully in touch. Sunrise and sunset, starlight and solstice. Times to slow down, and times to speed up. No time to waste, and yet, and *yet* … this precious and unrepeatable moment, here and now, is but the overflow of the unfathomable well-spring of deep time, and deep love.

Lower your bucket, raise your glass, drink your fill.

Cheers again.

We recall the paths that have led us into new territory, literally and metaphorically. Sometimes steep, sometimes flat, sometimes buried in mud or blocked by a fallen tree, occasionally hard to trace, or requiring tenacity just to keep on going.

There are the people we've bumped into along the way, usually offering a welcome smile and a cheery hello and an opportunity to share – and thus to amplify and multiply – the moment.

And there are those who have blazed a trail before us. We're part of a community – a communion of saints! – and we feel we've really *walked* with Edward Thomas and so many others, who feel present around our table now.

Here, the soulful wonder of Jeffries, and the open notebook of White as he captures a few fresh sightings; the fossil hunter Mary Anning pulls out a piece of rock and shares it so carefully with her progeny Steve Etches. Here's to them, and all the poets and writers and thinkers and artists who enrich our daily life with their presence; even though they are, in a sense, gone from here, they have walked with us, and continue to do so.

Here's to the places, the parishes, the people who have maintained those sacramental human rites of ordinary and often painful life, steadfastly, and brought us to this point. The love and the laughter and the tears of it all.

Here's to the healing that has happened along the way, sometimes slowly, sometimes all of a sudden, beneath a yew, or while watching the waves. Those mysterious moments of restoration, or gentle awakening; of new growth, ripeness, and fruitfulness, all of which remind us that we are organic, and that matter *matters*; we are born of this Earth as well as born of God and of our family.

Part of the interwoven whole, the ecosystem of love.

Here's to the old trees, and the new growth. To the broken branches and the scars that are left and the moss and the lichens and the fungi and the mulch and that smell of church within the hollowed-out places. To the birds that will nest and the insects that will swarm, and to the roots that hold fast and the trunk that gives strength and the leaves that will once again reach out to welcome in translucence the return of the great light of life to this Earth.

And here's to you, for you are part of the beauty of this place, this home, and without you it just would not be the same.

Cheers.

May the road rise up to meet you.

Go well!

Brian and Howard

Bibliography

Books and articles, by chapter

Introduction

Gerald May, *The Wisdom of Wilderness: Experiencing the Healing Power of Nature* (HarperOne, 2006)

1 January

Thomas Berry, *Evening Thoughts: Reflecting on Earth as Sacred Community* (Sierra Club Books, 2006)

Thomas Berry (Mary Evelyn Tucker, ed.), *Selected Writings on the Earth Community* (Orbis, 2014)

T. S. Eliot, *Four Quartets* (London: Faber and Faber, 2001)

Joanna Macy and Chris Johnstone, *Active Hope: How to Face the Mess We're in Without Going Crazy* (New World Library, 2012)

John McPhee, *Basin and Range* (Farrar, Strauss and Giroux, 1982)

Pierre Teilhard de Chardin (Ursula King, ed.), *Writings* (Orbis, 1999)

Pierre Teilhard de Chardin, as quoted in Michael Harter (ed.), *Hearts on Fire: Praying with Jesuits* (Loyola Press, 2005)

2 February

Jean-Henri Fabre, *The Life of the Fly* (translated: Fredonia Books, 2001)

Francis of Assisi, *Little Flowers of St Francis* (1390; this edition Cosimo Classics, 2007)

Richard Mabey, *Gilbert White: A Biography of the Author of The Natural History of Selborne* (Profile Books, 2006)

Robert Macfarlane, *Landmarks* (Hamish Hamilton, 2015)

Erica McAlister, *The Secret Life of Flies* (The Natural History Museum, 2017)

Edward Thomas, *The South Country* (1909; this edition Little Toller, 2009)

Gilbert White, *The Natural History and Antiquities of Selborne* (1788–9; this edition Penguin Classics, 1987)

3 March

Simon Barnes, *How to Be a Bad Birdwatcher: to the Greater Glory of Life*, (Short Books, 2006)

Paul Hindle, *Medieval Roads and Tracks* (Shire Archaeology, 2008)

Joanna Macy and Chris Johnstone, *Active Hope: How to Face the Mess We're in Without Going Crazy* (New World Library, 2012)

William D. McMaster, *Forest Man*, www.youtube.com/watch?v=H-kZDSqyE1do

Michael McCarthy, 'Mere Science Cannot Account for Beauty', *Independent* newspaper, 25 March 2011

Rainer Maria Rilke, 'The Ninth Duino Elegy', Stephen Mitchel, ed., *Duino Elegies and the Sonnets to Orpheus* (Vintage Books, 2010)

John O'Donohue, *Divine Beauty: The Invisible Embrace* (Harper-Collins, 2004)

Mary Oliver, 'At the River Clarion', in *Evidence* (Bloodaxe Books, 2009)

Barry Shurlock, *Walks in Wessex: The Test Way and the Clarendon Way* (Hampshire County Council, 1986)

Eckhart Tolle, *Oneness With All Life* (Michael Joseph, 2008)

Jean Watt's poem 'Lent' is found in Janet Morley, *The Heart's Time: A Poem a Day for Lent and Easter* (SPCK, 2011)

4 April

William Cobbett, *Rural Rides* (1830; this edition Penguin Classics, 2001)

Matthew Hollis, *Now All Roads Lead to France: The Last Years of Edward Thomas* (Faber & Faber, 2011)

Anne Lamott, *Help, Thanks, Wow: The Three Essential Prayers* (Riverhead, 2013)

Raimon Panikkar, *Christophany: The Fullness of Man* (Orbis, 2004)

Edward Thomas, *Collected Poems* (1920; this edition Faber & Faber, 2004)

Edward Thomas, *In Pursuit of Spring* (1914; this edition Little Toller, 2016)

Edward Thomas, *The South Country* (1909; this edition Little Toller, 2009)

5 May

Elizabeth Barrett Browning, *Aurora Leigh* (1856; this edition Oxford University Press, 2008)

Damian Carrington, 'Two-hour "dose" of nature significantly boosts health – study', *Guardian* newspaper, 13 June 2019

Simon Cooper, *Life of a Chalkstream* (William Collins, 2014)

Thich Nhat Hanh, 'The Practice of Mindfulness' (www.lionsroar.com)

John Lewis-Stemple, *Meadowland: The Private Life of an English Field* (Black Swan, 2015)

John O'Donohue, *To Bless the Space Between Us: A Book of Blessings* (Convergent Books, 2008)

Mary Oliver, *Upstream: Selected Essays* (Random House, 2016)

'One Million Species at Risk of Extinction, UN Report Warns', National Geographic website 2019 (www.nationalgeographic.co.uk). This references the report from the Intergovernmental Science-Policy Platform on Biodiversity and Ecosystem Services, 'Global Assessment Report on Biodiversity and Ecosystem Services' (2019)

Rebecca Solnit, *Savage Dreams: A Journey into the Landscape Wars of the American West* (Sierra Club Books, 1994)

Robin Wall Kimmerer, *Braiding Sweetgrass: Indigenous Wisdom, Scientific Knowledge and the Teaching of Plants* (Milkweed, 2015)

6 June

Wendell Berry, 'How to Be a Poet', in *New Collected Poems* (Counterpoint, 2013)

Richard Mabey, *Flora Britannica* (Chatto & Windus, 1996)

Michael McCarthy, *The Moth Snowstorm: Nature and Joy* (John Murray, 2016)

John O'Donohue, *Anam Cara: Wisdom from the Celtic World* (Bantam, 1999)

Parker J. Palmer, *Let Your Life Speak: Listening for the Voice of Vocation* (Jossey Bass, 1999)

Oliver Rackham, *The History of the Countryside* (Phoenix Press, 2000)

William Tyndale's translation of the Bible can be viewed at www.biblestudytools.com/tyn

7 *July*

Walter Besant, *The Eulogy of Richard Jefferies* (Chatto & Windus, 1888)

Mihaly Csikszentmihalyi, *Flow* (Rider, 2002)

Ram Dass and Mirabai Bush, *Walking Each Other Home: Conversations on Loving and Dying* (Sounds True, 2018)

Annie Dillard, *Pilgrim at Tinker Creek* (Canterbury Press, 2011)

Richard Jefferies, *Wild Life in a Southern County* (1878; this edition Little Toller, 2011)

Robert Macfarlane, *The Old Ways: A Journey on Foot* (Viking, 2012)

Martin and Nigel Palmer, *Sacred Britain: A Guide to the Sacred Sites and Pilgrim Routes of England, Scotland and Wales* (Piatkus, 1997)

Christopher Taylor, *Roads and Tracks of Britain* (J. M. Dent & Sons, 1979)

Edward Thomas, *Beautiful Wales* (1905)

Jane Upchurch, *A Leaf Between My Toes: Finding Wonder* (Onwards & Upwards, 2003)

Francis Weller, *The Wild Edge of Sorrow: Rituals of Renewal and the Sacred Work of Grief* (North Atlantic Books, 2015)

8 *August*

Wendell Berry, *Leavings: Poems* (Counterpoint Press, 2011)

Emily Cleaver, 'Against All Odds, England's Massive Chalk Horse Has Survived 3,000 Years' (www.smithsonian.com, 2017)

Ellis Davidson, 'Weland the Smith', *Folklore* 69.3 (1958)

Richard Hamblyn, *Extraordinary Clouds: Skies of the Unexpected from the Beautiful to the Bizarre* (David & Charles, 2009)

Ceri Houlbrook, 'The Penny's Dropped: Renegotiating the Contemporary Coin Deposit', *The Journal of Material Culture*, 2015

Richard Jefferies, *Round About a Great Estate* (1880; this edition Wentworth Press, 2019)

Richard Jefferies, *The Amateur Poacher* (1879; this edition Echo Books, 2005)

Richard Jefferies, *The Story of My Heart: My Autobiography* (1883; this edition Green Books, 2002)

Richard Jefferies, *Wild Life in a Southern County* (1878; this edition Little Toller, 2011)

Gavin Pretor-Pinney, 'Cloudy With a Chance of Joy', TED talk 2013 (www.ted.com)

Francis Wise citation from *The National Cyclopaedia of Useful Knowledge* (1847) via Wikipedia

9 September

Frederick Buechner, *Now and Then: A Memoir of Vocation* (Harper-Collins, 1983)

Annie Dillard, *Pilgrim at Tinker Creek* (Canterbury Press, 2011)

Daniel Ladinsky, 'The Sun Never Says', a poem taken from *The Gift: Poems By Hafiz* (Penguin, 1999)

John O'Donohue, *To Bless the Space Between Us* (Bantam, 1999)

Parker J. Palmer, *Let Your Life Speak: Listening for the Voice of Vocation* (Jossey Bass, 1999)

Francis Weller, *The Wild Edge of Sorrow: Rituals of Renewal and the Sacred Work of Grief* (North Atlantic Books, 2015)

10 October

Jane Austen, *Northanger Abbey* and *Persuasion* (John Murray, 1818)

Cynthia Bourgeault, *The Wisdom Way of Knowing: Reclaiming an Ancient Tradition to Awaken the Heart* (Jossey Bass, 2003)

John Gerard, *Gerard's Herbal* (1597; this edition Bracken Books, 1985)

John Keats, *The Collected Poems* (Penguin Classics, 1977)

Ann Lewin, *Watching for the Kingfisher: Poems and Prayers* (Inspire, 2004)

Robert Macfarlane and Jackie Morris, *The Lost Words: A Spell Book* (Hamish Hamilton, 2017)

John Philip Newell, *Christ of the Celts: The Healing of Creation* (Wild Goose, 2008)

D'Arcy Wentworth Thompson, *On Growth and Form* (Cambridge University Press, 1961)

11 November

Thomas Berry, *Evening Thoughts* (Sierra Club Books, 2006)

Thomas Berry, *The Sacred Universe: Earth, Spirit, and Religion in the Twenty-First Century* (Columbia University Press, 2009)

Elizabeth Gilbert, *Big Magic: Creative Living Beyond Fear* (Bloomsbury, 2015)

Geoffrey Grigson, *The Englishman's Flora* (1955; this edition J. M. Dent & Sons, 1987)

W. H. Hudson, *Nature in Downland* (1901; this edition Little, Brown, 1981)

Gerald May, *The Wisdom of Wilderness: Experiencing the Healing Power of Nature* (HarperOne, 2006)

John Philip Newell, *Christ of the Celts: The Healing of Creation* (Wild Goose, 2008)

John O'Donohue, *Eternal Echoes: Exploring Our Hunger to Belong* (Bantam Books, 2000)

12 December

Thomas Berry, *Evening Thoughts* (Sierra Club Books, 2006)

Barbara Brown Taylor, *Learning to Walk in the Dark* (Canterbury Press, 2014)

Abraham Joshua Heschel, *God in Search of Man: A Philosophy of Judaism* (1955; this edition Farrar, Straus and Giroux, 1976)

Patrick Kavanagh, 'Advent', *Collected Poems*, Antoinette Quin, ed. (Allen Lane, 2004)

Madeleine L'Engle, 'A Sky Full of Children', in *Watch for the Light: Readings for Advent and Christmas* (Plough Publishing, 2014)

Eugene H. Peterson, *The Message: The Bible in Contemporary Language* (NavPress, 2003)

Alexander Shaia, 'The Mythic Power of Christmas', speaking on The RobCast (www.robbell.com), 10 December, 2017

Quote from The Wildlife Trusts' Living Landscapes project via www.wildlifetrusts.org

Websites

www.ancient-yew.org

www.bbc.co.uk/news/science-environment-48827490

www.buglife.org.uk/

www.butterfly-conservation.org

www.hants.gov.uk

www.naturescalendar.woodlandtrust.org.uk

www.richardjefferies.org/

www.wilderness.org/

www.wildlifetrusts.org

Appendix

Finding the Twelve Walks

JANUARY: The Jurassic Coast, Kimmeridge and the Purbeck Hills, Dorset

Part 1: Ordnance Survey (OS) Explorer map, OL15. Map reference for Kimmeridge: SY917799. Postcode: BH20 5PE.

The main routes to Kimmeridge are either via Poole, Studland and Corfe from the east (but check that the Studland Ferry is running), or via Wareham from the west and the north. There is car parking at the Etches Collection, the Museum of Jurassic Marine Life, in the centre of Kimmeridge village, and also at Kimmeridge Bay. The final part of the road to Kimmeridge Bay has a toll at busier times. The walk from Kimmeridge village to the Bay and back is about two miles.

Part 2: Map reference for Stonehill Down Nature Reserve, Purbeck Hills: SY931820.

Leaving Kimmeridge and driving north to Stonehill Down, you may need to use the lanes to the east (rather than west past the village of Steeple), if the Army Firing Ranges are in use. Park at Cocknowle overlooking Stonehill Down and then walk west along Ridgeway Hill for some magnificent views of the Jurassic Coast and Kimmeridge Bay.

FEBRUARY: Selborne, Hampshire

OS Explorer map, OL33. Map reference for Selborne: SU743335. Postcode: GU34 3JR.

Nearest major roads are the A31 and A3. Follow signs to Selborne on the B3006. Parking is available behind the Selborne Arms in the middle of the High Street. Our walk goes up the Zig-Zag Path behind the car park, explores Selborne Common and then returns to walk around the valley to Priory Farm which is on the other side of the High Street behind St Mary's Church. Helpful websites include the National Trust for Selborne Common and East Hampshire District Council on Literary Walks in East Hampshire (Rev. Gilbert White). If you would like to combine this walk with the Edward Thomas walk at Steep (see April), the Hangers Way joins them up.

MARCH: Great Copse, Mottisfont, Hampshire

OS Explorer map, 131. Map reference for Great Copse car park: SU321283. Postcode for National Trust Mottisfont car park: SO51 OLP.

The nearest main road is the A3057 between Romsey and Andover. Drive past the National Trust's main car park and through the village. Carry straight on along Oakley Road and in about half a mile turn left into Back Lane. The car park for Great Copse is a short distance up Back Lane on the right. We walked anti-clockwise around the footpaths in Great Copse but there are several other paths through the wood. If you are in the area for more than a day, there is also an Estate Walk of about six miles which passes through several other woods managed by the National Trust. If you choose to walk to Great Copse from the main visitor car park at Mottisfont Abbey, we suggest that you follow the relevant section of the Estate Walk, via the Test Way and passing Queen Meadow Copse, rather than use the lanes which are narrow, winding and have steep verges.

APRIL: Steep near Petersfield, Hampshire

Part 1, Main walk: OS Explorer map, OL33. Map reference for All Saints Church, Steep: SU746254. Postcode: GU32 2DF.

The village of Steep is just off the junction of the A3 and A272. The walk starts at All Saints Church and there is parking along the adjacent road. The route that we followed can be found on East Hampshire District Council's website under Literary Walks in East Hampshire (Edward Thomas). It can also be combined with the walk around Selborne (February) and linked via the long-distance footpath, the Hangers Way.

Part 2, Visit to the White Horse Inn: Map reference: SU715290. Postcode: GU32 1DA.

As it does not have a sign, the White Horse is known locally as 'The Pub With No Name'. Edward Thomas regularly walked the considerable distance from Steep to the pub for a drink and a smoke of his beloved pipe. It still has a friendly atmosphere and good hospitality, if you have time for some refreshment at the end of the walk.

MAY: Mottisfont Abbey and its estate near Romsey, Hampshire

OS Explorer map, 131. Map reference for the National Trust Mottisfont car park: SU328268. Postcode: SO51 0LP.

On entering the grounds of Mottisfont Abbey, you cross a small brick bridge over the Abbey Stream where you can usually see several large brown trout. Pause and enjoy the magnificent trees and fine views of the house across the south lawn. Turn left and walk alongside the shady stream to the spring (or font) that gave Mottisfont its name ('meeting place by a spring'). Continue across the main drive and the paddock towards a circle of beech trees and then through a gate into the meadow.

Enjoy the views northwards up the Test Valley and the sights and sounds of the meadow.

Maybe take the opportunity to have some refreshments at one of the cafés before heading off for the longer section of the walk. Leaving your car in the visitor car park (which closes at 5.00pm in the main season; 4.00pm in the winter), turn right and with care walk through Mottisfont village and straight along Oakley Road to the Test Way footpath on the right at su325273. Follow the Test Way to Oakley Lane, turning left along the lane for about a quarter of a mile and then right along a signposted track to Queen Meadow Copse. Walk around the perimeter fence of the wood which is now coppiced for charcoal burning.

Retrace your steps back to Oakley Lane, turn left and continue past the gate to the Test Way and on about 100 metres to a bridge over the Oakley Stream. Cross the bridge and pause at the gravel track immediately on the left. This is a private track but you will see the Mottisfont Oak just to the right in a small field opposite Oakley Farm. Walk back to the gate for the Test Way and retrace your steps to Mottisfont village and the National Trust car park.

Mottisfont Abbey and village can also be accessed by train to Mottisfont and Dunbridge station (on the Southampton to Salisbury line) and then by following the National Trust signs for about one mile over the River Dun and across the fields to Mottisfont.

JUNE: Pepperbox Hill and Salisbury

The summer solstice, or longest day of the year, is usually on 21 June and we chose to meet for this month's walk on that date. If possible, we would encourage you to watch the sunrise and the sunset at a vantage point near your home. For directions to Stockbridge Down, please refer to our December directions below.

Part 1, Visit to Pepperbox Hill overlooking Salisbury: OS Explorer map, 131. Map reference: SU211249. Postcode: SP5 3QL.

Pepperbox Hill is located alongside the A36 about five miles south of Salisbury. There is a National Trust car park up a steep, narrow lane (but no toilets or refreshments). The hilltop is a nature reserve notable for the flora and fauna of chalk grassland. Enjoy the fine views in all directions, particularly across the Wiltshire Downs to the spire of Salisbury Cathedral in the distance, but also the intriguing lookout, the 'pepper-box' itself.

Part 2, Salisbury: OS Explorer map 130 covers Salisbury and the surrounding area including Old Sarum (the site of the original town) and Stonehenge (both now managed by English Heritage). Postcodes: for the long-stay car park: SP1 3SL; for the Visitor Information Centre (in Fish Row) and a city map: SP1 1EJ. Salisbury also has Park and Ride car parks. Another option is to travel to Salisbury by train; the station is less than a mile from the city centre.

We explored the Cathedral Close and then walked out from the city centre through Queen Elizabeth Gardens to the Town Path across the water meadows to the Old Mill and then returned. There are lots of other walking routes through the green spaces of this beautiful place. Evensong at the Cathedral is usually at 5.30pm on weekdays.

JULY: The Harroway, Hampshire

OS Explorer map, 144. Postcode for Overton village: RG25 3HG. Map reference for the lay-by on the Harrow Way: SU514517.

Turn off the A34 at Whitchurch and on to the B3400, driving east along the Test Valley to Overton. Turn left in the centre of Overton and up the hill towards Kingsclere. The lay-by on the Harrow Way is about one mile north at the map reference above. We walked east along the Harrow Way, then retraced our steps, crossing the road at the lay-by and walking westwards for a mile or so. Various diversions and extensions are possible so you can make this walk your own.

There is the option on this walk of visiting the source of the River Test. To do this: return to the centre of Overton, turn left and drive for about one mile to the hamlet of Ashe. Park by the church and follow the footpath westwards. In a short distance there is a muddy pond to the left (marked as the source of the Test on the OS Explorer map) and a stream that winds its way across a field, although it was dried up when we visited. This is as close as we got to the source of the Test but at Overton, about one mile downstream, the river has already become a bubbling, crystal-clear brook with small trout lurking among the weeds.

AUGUST: Coate, Wiltshire, and the Ridgeway, Oxfordshire/Berkshire border

Part 1, Richard Jefferies Museum at Coate, Swindon, Wiltshire: OS Explorer map, 169. Map reference: SU179829. Postcode: SN3 6AA.

Exit junction 15 on the M4 motorway and drive north to the roundabout on the A419 for the A4259. Turn left; a short distance along this dual carriageway, the Richard Jefferies Museum is on the left, a thatched farmhouse surrounded by Coate Water Country Park and new housing developments for south-east Swindon. Check opening times on the museum website.

Part 2: Uffington, the Ridgeway and the White Horse on the Oxfordshire/Berkshire border: OS Explorer map, 170. Map reference: SU294866. Postcode for National Trust car park: SN7 7QJ.

Return to the roundabout on the A419 and cross to the B4507, passing through Upper Wanborough and Bishopstone. At the junction for Woolstone turn right, following signs to the National Trust car park for Uffington Castle and the White Horse. Walk the short distance uphill to the Ridgeway and explore this ancient track to the west for Wayland's Smithy and to the east for Uffington Castle and the White Horse. You can make this walk as long as you like but do pause regularly to enjoy the wonderful skyscapes and the magnificent views.

SEPTEMBER: Romsey, Hampshire

OS Explorer map, 131. Map reference for the Information Centre (Church Street) in Romsey and a town map: SU352213. Postcode: SO51 8BT. There are several long-stay car parks near the centre of Romsey. The town can also be accessed by regular train services from Salisbury, Southampton and beyond.

We suggest that you prepare for this walk by thinking about the wildlife that lives in your own town and its green spaces, including the humble pigeon. Use the town map for Romsey to see the splendid horse chestnut tree by the library and to explore the garden of King John's House; Romsey Abbey and its surrounds; Wisdom House and the labyrinth (just opposite the junction of The Abbey and The Meads); the War Memorial Park with the war horse statue and Sadler's Mill on the River Test. As you walk, spot the 'Poetry in Motion' plaques on the pavements and walls of the town centre.

Return to the town centre and, if you have time (or on another visit), head north along Station Road and the Canal Walk to Fishlake Meadows Nature Reserve. This is an area of wetland now owned by Test Valley Borough Council and managed by the Hampshire and Isle of Wight Wildlife Trust. Rare birds like the great white egret, osprey, marsh harrier and Cetti's warbler are either regular visitors or residents. Otters and water voles are well established. The Reserve is a precious asset for a small town in the south of England.

OCTOBER: Winchester and St Catherine's Hill, Hampshire

OS Explorer map, OL32. Map reference for the Cathedral Close: SU481292. Postcode: SO23 9LS. Winchester has several Park and Ride car parks and the Cathedral Close is less than a mile from the railway station. The Visitor Information Centre is at the Guildhall in the High Street, postcode: SO23 9GH.

Our walk starts in the Cathedral Close, passes under the King's Gate into College Street and then follows the wall of Winchester College, turning right and then left into College Walk. It then crosses the Black Bridge over the River Itchen and turns right to join the Itchen Way southwards into the water meadows adjoining the Itchen Navigation and the College's playing fields. At the first road crossing, turn left and ascend St Catherine's Hill for panoramic views of the city and surrounding countryside. Retrace this route and, if you would like to attend evensong at the cathedral, it is usually at 5.30pm on weekdays.

NOVEMBER: Kingley Vale National Nature Reserve, near Chichester, West Sussex

OS Explorer map: OL8. Map reference for the car park at Kingley Vale NNR, West Stoke: SZ825088. Postcode: PO18 9BN.

Kingley Vale NNR is in a fold of the South Downs just a short drive north-west of Chichester. There are numerous footpaths in the area and a trail on the Visit Chichester website. We walked from the car park at West Stoke northwards along a track directly into the nature reserve. The grove of ancient yew trees is on the right of the valley bottom, followed by the dew pond, a steep ascent to the ridge of the South Downs and the Arthur Tansley Memorial Stone. Walking poles might be helpful on this walk as the steep part of the track can get muddy. Our main purpose was not to visit Chichester but it is nearby and another beautiful city.

DECEMBER: Stockbridge Down, near Stockbridge, Hampshire

OS Explorer map: 131. Map reference for the National Trust car park at Stockbridge Down (nearest Stockbridge, see below): SU375346. Postcode: SO28 8EG.

The National Trust car parks for Stockbridge Down are alongside the B3049, Winchester to Stockbridge road. The references above are for the car park at the west end of the Down, nearer Stockbridge. There is another car park at the east end. The National Trust website has further information about the wildlife and management of Stockbridge Down. There are many footpaths and extensive grassland to wander. The highest point is the rampart of Woolbury Ring, an Iron Age hill fort, with spectacular views in all directions. As some of the paths up to Woolbury are steep and can be muddy in the winter, walking poles may be a helpful aid for the ascent. Aim to be at the west side of the Down for the sunset which is at about 4.00 pm on the shortest day (21 December).